PREFERENCES

PREFERENCES

51 American poets
choose poems from their own work
and from the past

commentary on the choices
and an introduction by
RICHARD HOWARD

photographs of the poets by
THOMAS VICTOR

THE VIKING PRESS · NEW YORK

Contents

Introduction

Miss Wickwire—Miss Gail Wickwire, who taught the College Preparatory English classes at Shaker Heights High School—had lovely arms and a problem. They appeared at about the same time in the spring term: no sooner were the Victorian poets "done" than sleeves withdrew to the shoulders and there was the problem—the Modern Poets. We did not know who they were—we were in her classroom to learn—but Miss Wickwire knew, she knew a problem when she saw one. She knew who the Moderns, as she called them, were; she recognized them because they were different, altogether different from the Victorians and the Romantics and the Elizabethans she had "taught" us. Perhaps they were not so different from the Metaphysical Poets, nor from the Mad Poets at the end of the eighteenth century, but neither metaphysics nor madness buttered much hay with Miss Wickwire, who also taught us (as long as the snow was on the ground) *The Return of the Native*. The Moderns (and was not Hardy one of them?) were altogether different from the poets it was her responsibility to expound—yet here was a novel, not quite a Victorian novel, was it? by one of them: might there not be some means of getting from one category to the other across that lugubrious bridge *The Return of the Native*, of proceeding from the peregrine Moderns to the permeable Victorians and thence to the Roman-tics and so forth, or so back? No—here Miss Wickwire flung out her arms in a pretty gesture of despair, there was nothing to be done: she stood, in short sleeves, on one side of a trench with Shakespeare and Shelley and even with Eustacia Vye; and on the other side, the Modern side, loomed those mysterious poets, disaffected, alien, dumb.

Twenty years after my first glimpse of that trench, I had occasion myself to teach an in-service course to high-school English teachers of New York City. "Contemporary Poets" our course was called, and indeed each week a different contemporary poet sat beside me on the dais while I expounded his poems, her poems, and the teachers took a lot of notes. How different, these teachers often told me and the poet in question, how different contemporary poetry was from all the poetry they taught their own students—how difficult and how painful, how demanding and how unpleasant. Contemporary poetry, they concluded, was a problem. Not only Miss Wickwire, then, but many others whose business it was to know something about poetry, and furthermore who went about their business with a great deal of good will, a good deal of gratitude for small favors (such as discovering that the Contemporary Poet did not regard himself as a problem), stood even now on one side of that same trench—was it not in fact a canyon, the Great Divide which opened up within literature about 1900, or say 1914?—and on the farther shore loomed against us, ever more numerous, the Modern Poets, though scarcely numerous enough to "count" against the ranks of the past which were *with us*: the Elizabethan Poets, the Victorian Poets, the Romantic Poets, even the Metaphysical Poets (for this was Manhattan, where the Metaphysicals were taught in high school, though *The Return of the Native* had given way, it is my impression, to *The Catcher in the Rye*).

A poet was modern, then, if he suffered or sustained an apparent division from the poetry of the past, and all the more modern if he insisted on the appearances of that division. His insistence in matters of form could be particularly ominous, for matters of form were so much more than merely that—were so very distinctive in poetry. The Great Divide, I realized, was part of the geology of our reading life; that is, it did not mean the same thing to say "I read poetry by my contemporaries" as it meant to say "I read Wordsworth and Donne and Hopkins and Smart." It meant, really, *I have a taste for the problematic*; whereas the reader of those poets Miss Wickwire stood with or stood for—that reader was assumed to have a taste for, merely, poetry. Poetry—the poetry of Hopkins or Donne or Smart—was not problematic, unless of course you began to read it the way you read modern poetry.

There was the solution to Miss Wickwire's problem, if she had known it: so great is the retroactive power of the present, so incomparable our own modernity, that in its light we shall see all the work of the past transformed. The Moderns will change the way we read the Victorians, the Romantics, the Elizabethans, and all those others. And they had better: if we cannot read our contemporaries, then we cannot read our classics—we can only revere them as works whose reputation is so great that no one can earn much credit by praising them, and so vague that no one can earn much credit by attacking them.

Yet, as Randall Jarrell used to say, it is always in the name of the easy past that we condemn the difficult present. It is only when we can bring ourselves to acknowledge that everything —past and present alike—is difficult that everything becomes, in fact, easy. The solution to Miss Wickwire's problem was to reverse the terms—to regard precisely those features of a poem, of a poetry, which trouble us as the ones which, if we yield to them, if we treat them as significance rather than as defect, will turn out to be answers to what we had regarded as "problems" of composition and utterance.

Judging by my own experience, it is time—and with the time comes this occasion—that we stop being educated by our classics and begin reading them—just as we may stop being outraged or bored or provoked or offended by our contemporaries and begin using them—allowing them—to educate us.

When Thomas Victor showed me some of his photographs of contemporary poets and proposed an anthology of preferences by them and by other poets—poems of their own they preferred, and with them poems from the past, poems from before 1900, from the entire range of poetry with which they felt their own poems sustained some interesting relation, even the relation of contradiction or challenge—I knew that he had afforded me a means of traversing that trench. Perhaps by no more than a few planks across the Great Divide, yet of Division as of Tyranny, Péguy's remark holds true: its victory lasts but a moment though its ruins may be eternal. By making this anthology of preferences I could leave the ruins of misunderstanding and neglect around me where they had fallen, but I could bridge the trench with whatever might come my way of attention and discernment in the form of commentary, of critical illumination. The point was not to get *the poets* to speak for continuities, to avow interferences, even contaminations, but to find them for myself, to discover—as others, beguiled by the paired poems, by Mr. Victor's unmediated images, would have occasion to discover—that the writing of poetry is one enterprise, continuous, seamless, not to be called off after 1900 or 1914, not to be called into being as if it had not possessed the minds and hearts and lungs and senses of men and women since first there were men and women. The poetry keeps being written—and the trench keeps being moved.

Therefore Tom Victor and I asked fifty poets of an extremely wide range—poets who were, in fact, alive in 1900, or writing in 1914, as well as poets born since 1940 (surely *they* were Modern Poets), to select, to *prefer* in their own work and in the work of the past a pair of poems of feasible length which they saw fit to put together, which, in some sense, fit. The preferences are before you, and they too range very widely. Twenty years ago, had the choices been made by the poets coeval with Miss Wickwire, there would have been many more Metaphysicals (though there are a number, even so); the choice here of so many nineteenth-century poems is a phenomenon which would surprise the graduate student of the nineteen-fifties. And the appearance of a number of Poets of Sensibility, as Northrop Frye has suggested we call the "mad" poets of the late eighteenth century, would perhaps interest the student of fashion in these affairs. But it is the individual poems which interest me, the individual choices, the preferences of each poet as they came, with their enforced horizons of relevance, of relation, of relish: the physiognomy of preference, one might say. And with the preferences came the photographs, the astonishment of Tom Victor's talent to back me up, to lead me on. For the physiognomies *he* revealed had so little in them of his own imposing, so much in them of his subjects only, that his images loom for me on the far side of a trench of my own—as a model of interpretation, of illumination; in Tom Victor's photographs, the subject is led—beguiled, seduced, the tactics are inconceivable—to disclose himself without the interposition of Mr. Victor's preferences. Tom Victor is the servant of his vision, and he lets that lens clarify us all. I have sought to do as much, and with a like acknowledgment that what I see is not all there is to see or say, but rather what may be seen and said at this angle, from this point of view, by these lights.

It would have pleased us to include poets whom we invited to appear in the book but who declined. It would have pleased us to include many more poets we have not invited because our publisher's deadlines and our own energies respectively mounted and waned. We thank all the poets who have collaborated so handsomely in the project (the versions of the poems of the past are their own preferences too), and I should like to add here a note of thanks to Miss Wickwire, whose failure was only part of my future, and whose endeavor was, after all, no different from what my own has been, from what the word *endeavor* literally means: an obligation, a debt to art.

A. R.
Ammons

GRAVELLY RUN

I don't know somehow it seems sufficient
to see and hear whatever coming and going is,
losing the self to the victory
      of stones and trees,
of bending sandpit lakes, crescent
round groves of dwarf pine:

for it is not so much to know the self
as to know it as it is known
      by galaxy and cedar cone,
as if birth had never found it
and death could never end it:

3

the swamp's slow water comes
down Gravelly Run fanning the long
    stone-held algal
hair and narrowing roils between
the shoulders of the highway bridge:

holly grows on the banks in the woods there,
and the cedars' gothic-clustered
    spires could make
green religion in winter bones:

so I look and reflect, but the air's glass
jail seals each thing in its entity:

no use to make any philosophies here:
    I see no
god in the holly, hear no song from
the snowbroken weeds: Hegel is not the winter
yellow in the pines: the sunlight has never
heard of trees: surrendered self among
    unwelcoming forms: stranger,
hoist your burdens, get on down the road.

Ralph Waldo Emerson

—

THE SNOW-STORM

Announced by all the trumpets of the sky,
Arrives the snow, and, driving o'er the fields,
Seems nowhere to alight: the whited air
Hides hills and woods, the river, and the heaven,
and veils the farm-house at the garden's end.
The sled and traveller stopped, the courier's feet
Delayed, all friends shut out, the housemates sit
Around the radiant fireplace, enclosed
In a tumultuous privacy of storm.

Come see the north wind's masonry.
Out of an unseen quarry evermore
Furnished with tile, the fierce artificer
Curves his white bastions with projected roof
Round every windward stake, or tree, or door.
Speeding, the myriad-handed, his wild work
So fanciful, so savage, nought cares he
For number or proportion. Mockingly,
On coop or kennel he hangs Parian wreaths;
A swan-like form invests the hidden thorn;
Fills up the farmer's lane from wall to wall,
Maugre the farmer's sighs; and at the gate
A tapering turret overtops the work.
And when his hours are numbered, and the world
Is all his own, retiring, as he were not,
Leaves, when the sun appears, astonished Art
To mimic in slow structures, stone by stone,
Built in an age, the mad wind's night-work,
The frolic architecture of the snow.

Comment

"I am very much struck by the appearance that one person wrote all the books," Emerson noted; "literature is plainly the work of one all-seeing, all-hearing gentleman." Indeed, between Coleridge's "Frost at Midnight" and Frost's "Stopping by Woods on a Snowy Evening" (which *plainly* prefigures Emerson's "sled and traveller stopped"), the sumptuous inhumanities of "The Snow-Storm" constitute not only a middle term but an extremity as well, extreme in articulation of that Other we must live with and must die into, a limit-instance of that "mode of motion," as Ammons elsewhere calls it, which is all that is not ourselves.

Against it, or merely with it ("it"—labeled Nature or the north wind, as by Emerson here, or by Ammons "air's glass jail"), distinguished from *it*, all human endeavor and art are one, whatever their freakish particulars. "When me they fly, I am the wings," says Emerson's terrible voice of Otherness ("Brahma"), and it comes as no more than a shock of recognition that Ammons should answer or anticipate this in "What This Mode of Motion Said," a poem much anterior to "Gravelly Run": "I am the wings when you me fly," his voiced Being announces to mortality, distinctively altering the mode; for Ammons, our exquisite poet of address, speaks most assuredly in the vocative, forever apostrophizing himself, others, and that "it" which has never heard of trees, the universe.

Patience with particulars, submission and loyalty to finite being—these energies in a poet constitute a great resignation, even a greater renunciation, because there is that within us which would be infinite and therefore be nothing— make Ammons, like the Emerson he echoes and extends, capable of hoisting his burdens, likely to get on down the road, even as a stranger, for in his initiating aporia he has found (as Stevens prophesied when he said that "The mind is the great poem of winter, the man, / Who, to find what will suffice, / Destroys romantic tenements / Of rose and ice") *what will suffice*: "it seems sufficient / to see and hear whatever coming and going is," along with Emerson's all-seeing, all-hearing gentleman. It is the great quest of our poetry, such emptying-out, such ablation of our ideas that our identity may be revealed:

> *for it is not so much to know the self*
> *as to know it as it is known*
> > *by galaxy and cedar cone,*
> *as if birth had never found it*
> *and death could never end it.*

Ammons wrote that great music, but once written it is no longer just his. For every new writer, as Emerson wrote, is only a new crater of an old volcano.

John
Ashbery

SOONEST MENDED

Barely tolerated, living on the margin
In our technological society, we were always having to be rescued
On the brink of destruction, like heroines in *Orlando Furioso*
Before it was time to start all over again.
There would be thunder in the bushes, a rustling of coils
And Angelica, in the Ingres painting, was considering
The colorful but small monster near her toe, as though wondering whether forgetting
The whole thing might not, in the end, be the only solution.
And then there always came a time when
Happy Hooligan in his rusted green automobile
Came plowing down the course, just to make sure everything was O.K.,
Only by that time we were in another chapter and confused
About how to receive this latest piece of information.
Was it information? Weren't we rather acting this out
For someone else's benefit, thoughts in a mind
With room enough and to spare for our little problems (so they began to seem),
Our daily quandary about food and rent and bills to be paid?
To reduce all this to a small variant,
To step free at last, minuscule on the gigantic plateau—
This was our ambition: to be small and clear and free.
Alas, the summer's energy wanes quickly,
A moment and it is gone. And no longer
May we make the necessary arrangements, simple as they are.
Our star was brighter perhaps when it had water in it.
Now there is no question even of that, but only
Of holding on to the hard earth so as not to get thrown off,
With an occasional dream, a vision: a robin flies across
The upper corner of the window, you brush your hair away
And cannot quite see, or a wound will flash
Against the sweet faces of the others, something like:
This is what you wanted to hear, so why
Did you think of listening to something else? We are all talkers
It is true, but underneath the talk lies
The moving and not wanting to be moved, the loose
Meaning, untidy and simple like a threshing floor.

9

These then were some hazards of the course,
Yet though we knew the course *was* hazards and nothing else
It was still a shock when, almost a quarter of a century later,
The clarity of the rules dawned on you for the first time.
They were the players, and we who had struggled at the game
Were merely spectators, though subject to its vicissitudes
And moving with it out of the tearful stadium, borne on shoulders at last.
Night after night this message returns, repeated
In the flickering bulbs of the sky, raised past us, taken away from us,
Yet ours over and over until the end that is past truth,
The being of our sentences, in the climate that fostered them,
Not ours to own, like a book, but to be with, and sometimes
To be without, alone and desperate.
But the fantasy makes it ours, a kind of fence-sitting
Raised to the level of an esthetic ideal. These were moments, years,
Solid with reality, faces, namable events, kisses, heroic acts,
But like the friendly beginning of a geometrical progression
Not too reassuring, as though meaning could be cast aside some day
When it had been outgrown. Better, you said, to stay cowering
Like this in the early lessons, since the promise of learning
Is a delusion, and I agreed, adding that
Tomorrow would alter the sense of what had already been learned,
That the learning process is extended in this way, so that from this standpoint
None of us ever graduates from college,
For time is an emulsion, and probably thinking not to grow up
Is the brightest kind of maturity for us, right now at any rate.
And you see, both of us were right, though nothing
Has somehow come to nothing; the avatars
Of our conforming to the rules and living
Around the home have made—well, in a sense, "good citizens" of us,
brushing the teeth and all that, and learning to accept
The charity of the hard moments as they are doled out.
For this is action, this not being sure, this careless
Preparing, sowing the seeds crooked in the furrow,
Making ready to forget, and always coming back
To the mooring of starting out, that day so long ago.

Thomas Traherne

—

POVERTY

As in the House I sate
Alone and desolate,
No Creature but the Fire and I,
The Chimney and the Stool, I lift mine Ey
Up to the Wall
And in the Silent Hall
Saw nothing mine
But som few Cups and Dishes shine
The Table and the wooden Stools
Where Peeple us'd to dine:
A painted Cloth there was
Wherein som ancient Story wrought
A little entertain'd my Thought
Which Light discover'd throu the Glass.

I wonder'd much to see
That all my Wealth should be
Confin'd in such a little Room,
Yet hope for more I scarcely durst presume.
It griev'd me sore
That such a scanty Store
Should be my All:
For I forgat my Eas and Health,
Nor did I think of Hands or Eys,
Nor Soul nor Body prize;

I neither thought the Sun,
Nor Moon, nor Stars, nor Peeple, *mine*,
Tho they did round about me shine;
And therefore was I quite undon.

Som greater things I thought
Must nedes for me be wrought,
Which till my pleased Mind could see
I ever should lament my Poverty:
I fain would have
Whatever Bounty gave;
Nor could there be
Without, or Lov or Deity:
For, should not He be Infinit
Whose Hand created me?
Ten thousand absent things
Did vex my poor and absent Mind,
Which, till I be no longer blind,
Let me not see the King of Kings.

His Lov must surely be
Rich, infinit, and free;
Nor can He be thought a Gold
Of Grace and Pow'r, that fills not his Abode,
His Holy Court,
In kind and liberal sort;
Joys and Pleasures,
Plenty of Jewels, Goods, and Treasures,
(To enrich the Poor, cheer the forlorn)
His Palace must adorn,
And given all to me:
For till *His* Works *my* Wealth became,
No Lov, or Peace, did me enflame:
But now I have a DEITY.

Comment /

In a more recent poem than "Soonest Mended," one which will take much longer to mend for it is very much longer, in "The System" Ashbery has glossed his preference for Traherne's meditation on the sanctity of objects: "It is possible to know just enough, and this is all we were supposed to know. . . . We are to read this in outward things: the spoons and greasy tables in this room, the wooden shelves, the flyspecked ceiling merging into gloom—good and happy things, nevertheless, that tell us little of themselves and more about ourselves than we had ever imagined it was possible to know." Ashbery's more recent poem is in prose, of course, for both he and Traherne tend toward a poetics without the tension of negativity, without the invoked anxiety of a closed form; they are hampered by the necessity—it is *the* necessity of verse—of making ends meet. That is why Traherne never repeated a stanza pattern from one poem to another, and why Ashbery's lines run on, or peter out; they do not shore up the poem's energy by any kind of rhythmic or musical constant: the poem is endlessly obliging but under no obligation. Both poets are travelers, then, upon the Affirmative Way, which pursues perfection through delight in the created world. "Never," says Traherne, "was any thing in this World loved too much." Ashbery's way of loving the things of this world is not, by customary patterns and associations, to distort, to atrophy or distend what is—merely, but also marvelously—there. "A kind of fence-sitting / Raised to the level of an esthetic ideal" he calls it here, "For this is action, this not being sure, this careless / Preparing . . ." and indeed he does not wield language to convey the disciplinary, punitive passion which is the art's contribution and conventional resource. He means, and manages, to convince by letting things alone. His poem is already there, and what he calls "the secret of the search" is that its given, its constituted existence in the world, makes all choosing certain to succeed, and therefore eliminates the necessity of choice. The objective of the poem is not subjective, it is the poem's subject, and the poem's *meaning* is then in its making: "This banality which in the last analysis is our / Most precious possession, because allowing us / To rise above ourselves."

Perhaps it is only fair to conclude by letting Traherne gloss Ashbery, as one takes a square inch of some old master, enlarges it, and discovers the energetic realization of all modern art. "You never Enjoy the World aright," says this mysterious metaphysical whose very existence was not discerned, winnowed out of Vaughan, until 1903, "till the Sea it self floweth in your Veins, till you are Clothed with the Heavens, and crowned with the Stars: and Perceiv your self to be the Sole Heir of the whole World."

The aspiration here is that poems be not about, but that they *be* the world.

W. H.
Auden

IN DUE SEASON

Springtime, Summer and Fall: days to behold a world
Antecedent to our knowing, where flowers think
Theirs concretely in scent-colors and beasts, the same
Age all over, pursue dumb horizontal lives
On one level of conduct and so cannot be
Secretary to man's plot to become divine.

Lodged in all is a set metronome: thus, in May
Bird-babes still in the egg click to each other *Hatch!*;
June-struck cuckoos go off-pitch; when obese July
Turns earth's heating up, unknotting their poisoned ropes,
Vipers move into play; warned by October's nip,
Younger leaves to the old give the releasing draught.

Winter, though, has the right tense for a look indoors
At ourselves, and with First Names to sit face-to-face,
Time for reading of thoughts, time for the trying-out
Of new metres and new recipes, proper time
To reflect on events noted in warmer months
Till, transmuted, they take part in a human tale.

There, responding to our cry for intelligence,
Nature's mask is relaxed into a mobile grin,
Stones, old shoes, come alive, born sacramental signs,
Nod to us in the First Person of mysteries
They know nothing about, bearing a message from
The invisible sole Source of specific things.

Thomas Campion

WHAT FAIRE POMPE

What faire pompe have I spide of glittering Ladies;
With locks sparckled abroad, and rosie Coronet
On their yvorie browes, trackt to the daintie thies
With roabs like *Amazons*, blew as Violet,
With gold Aiglets adornd, some in a changeable
Pale; with spangs wavering taught to be moveable.

Then those Knights that a farre off with dolorous viewing
Cast their eyes hetherward; loe, in an agonie,
All unbrac'd, crie aloud, their heavie state ruing:
Moyst cheekes with blubbering, painted as *Ebonie*
Blacke; their feltred haire torne with wrathful hand:
And whiles astonied, starke in a maze they stand.

But hearke! what merry sound! what sodaine harmonie!
Looke looke neere the grove where the Ladies doe tread
With their Knights the measures waide by the melodie.
Wantons! whose travesing make men enamoured;
Now they faine an honor, now by the slender wast
He must lift hir aloft, and seale a kisse in hast.

Streight downe under a shadow for wearines they lie
With pleasant daliance, hand knit with arme in arme,
Now close, now set aloof, they gaze with an equall eie,
Changing kisses alike; streight with a false alarme,
Mocking kisses alike, powt with a lovely lip.
Thus drownd with jollities, their merry daies doe slip.

But stay! now I discerne they goe on a Pilgrimage
Towards Loves holy land, faire *Paphos* or *Cyprus*.
Such devotion is meete for a blithesome age;
With sweet youth, it agrees well to be amorous.
Let olde angrie fathers lurke in an Hermitage:
Come, weele associate this jolly Pilgrimage!

Comment

Horatian, he calls himself these days, not only in the selection of meter ("an attempt to write an English poem in the First Asclepiadean (spondee, choriamb, choriamb, iamb), the original model is Horace, *Odes*, Book I, no. 1"), but in the temper of his rejections ("enthusiastic / Youth writes you off as cold, who cannot be found on / Barricades, and never shoot / either yourselves or your lovers"—from "The Horatians," in the same collection as "In Due Season"). And it is so, the poetry comes now under the sign of a consented-to mortality, concerned with boundaries, limitations, precarious identifications which make our life possible—that naming which was Adam's first task and Auden's to the last. Here, miraculously taken up into verse, the gloss on Instructive Readings from Lorenz, Storrs, Bleibtreu, and Milnes, seasonable indeed and duly, even dutifully, concerned with appropriate acts for appropriate climes and times—like the Campion he chooses as companion-piece. But Auden's preference is deliberately a matter of movement, "the only other example in English verse that I know of," and worth some words from the man who recommends that young poets keep on their shelves Saintsbury's *History of English Prosody*: "The difference between Campion and me is that Campion could not decide whether to scan by vowel quantity or by stress: some lines do one, some another. Mine is purely accentual and ignores vowel length altogether." There is more, though, than metrical enthusiasm—metrical zealotry?—in the juxtaposition. There is the sense of *meete devotions*, the recognition that "With sweet youth, it agrees well to be amorous. / Let old angrie fathers lurke in an Hermitage." From that, one moves to Auden's syllabic line with just the right touch not of the tears but of the tide of things, the true Horation note: "Younger leaves to the old give the releasing draught."

17

Marvin
Bell

3 STANZAS ABOUT A TREE

1

The tree, too, wants to bend over
and wait a million years for an agate bridge
itself may have become, as we
turn and turn into, with final grace,
that seamless singleness we could not embody
across the river in our own bodies.

2

The tree has bent over which carried
us here, striations like glyphs from
who-could-imagine, and there were plenty,
too, who came for the sun,
who now are burnt into the earth
in a black seal familiar to but one or two.

3

Have we a vault for fury, a cathedral,
like the redwood? Have we wanted to be glass
or a diamond of the first water? That oak
has the same date with carbon we have.
Have I (think!) wanted to be the tree, or
one, two or three stanzas about a tree?

Emily Dickinson

—

JUST LOST, WHEN I WAS SAVED!

Just lost, when I was saved!
Just felt the world go by!
Just girt me for the onset with Eternity,
When breath blew back,
And on the other side
I heard recede the disappointed tide!

Therefore, as One returned, I feel
Odd secrets of the line to tell!
Some Sailor, skirting foreign shores—
Some pale Reporter, from the awful doors
Before the Seal!

Next time, to stay!
Next time, the things to see
By Ear unheard,
Unscrutinized by Eye—

Next time, to tarry,
While the Ages steal—
Slow tramp the Centuries,
And the Cycles wheel!

Comment

We are not intended to know, in the welter and rush of Dickinson's restoration to life—a period theme in an age of Interesting Deathbeds: compare it with Charlotte Brontë's version in *Villette*, Chapter 16—whether it is a welcome loss. Dickinson is exclamatory, Bell is interrogative about the escape from eschatology, but neither will assign value (poets don't) to the failure which is identified with survival. Loss is living, of course, but there are certain limit-experiences which suggest what gain might be, even "before the Seal" which is affixed in both poems, though naturally Bell proposes a naturalistic emblem for what is all capitalized reference in the pre-Darwinian Dickinson. We need not, though, subscribe to any particular rhetoric to recognize the occasion; it is one so central to our mortality as to turn incandescent any set of figures, however conventional, which are brought close to it—the receding tide, the river in our bodies. Envy of eternity is one of the great subjects, *flood subjects*, Dickinson called them, though the later poet must, with Blake, reverse the direction of the envy, must wonder if natural process accounts for hardening, for vitrifying, petrifying wood into "that seamless singleness we could not embody / across the river in our own bodies." . . . But what about our own lives, who cannot wait a million years to turn into an agate bridge? The agonizing questions Bell ends on ("Think!" he adjures himself parenthetically, as if that would do it) are the consequence of his realization that "the mind wants to dwell on the body" in every sense of the verb, there being no sense in eternity unless our senses make it. If poetry is what survives the self, what is the use of merely living? But doctrinal adherence aside, or underneath, both poets are committed to succession, not success. In their passages, no utterance is permitted to have its nodal resonance—it must simply, or sapiently, come again, onward and inward; so that Bell, in a sequence of fifty-four idiomorphic lyrics of which this is one of the last, may "scribble in the temporary / waters the line of greatest resistance"; and so that Dickinson, in the irregular outburst which is dated early on in her great torrent of five years' dissatisfaction with any one poem, may promise herself some potential life of identity ("secrets of the line") free of the past and not yet frozen into doom—"Next time, to stay! / Next time . . . ." Such poems, or rather such *poetry*, for there is no putting up with just poems here, is a search for what will suffice, forever starting up, unable to call a halt: loss is gain, we are blessed by creative anxieties which account for a life otherwise merely committed to endurance, submission, earth.

Elizabeth Bishop

IN THE WAITING ROOM

In Worcester, Massachusetts,
I went with Aunt Consuelo
to keep her dentist's appointment
and sat and waited for her
in the dentist's waiting room.
It was winter. It got dark
early. The waiting room
was full of grown-up people,
arctics and overcoats,
lamps and magazines.
My aunt was inside
what seemed like a long time
and while I waited I read
the *National Geographic*
(I could read) and carefully
studied the photographs:
The inside of a volcano,
black, and full of ashes;
then it was spilling over
in rivulets of fire.
Osa and Martin Johnson
dressed in riding breeches,
laced boots, and pith helmets.
A dead man slung on a pole
—"Long Pig," the caption said.
Babies with pointed heads
wound round and round with string;
black, naked women with necks
wound round and round with wire
like the necks of light bulbs.
Their breasts were horrifying.

I read it right straight through.
I was too shy to stop.
And then I looked at the cover:
the yellow margins, the date.

Suddenly, from inside,
came an *oh!* of pain
—Aunt Consuelo's voice—
not very loud or long.
I wasn't at all surprised;
even then I knew she was
a foolish, timid woman.
I might have been embarrassed,
but wasn't. What took me
completely by surprise
was that it was *me:*
my voice, in my mouth.
Without thinking at all
I was my foolish aunt,
I—we—were falling, falling,
our eyes glued to the cover
of the *National Geographic*,
February, 1918.

I said to myself: three days
and you'll be seven years old.
I was saying it to stop
the sensation of falling off
the round, turning world
into cold, blue-black space.

But I felt: you are an *I,*
you are an *Elizabeth,*
you are one of *them.*
Why should you be one, too?
I scarcely dared to look
to see what it was I was.
I gave a sidelong glance
—I couldn't look any higher—
at shadowy gray knees,
trousers and skirts and boots
and different pairs of hands
lying under the lamps.
I knew that nothing stranger
had ever happened, that nothing
stranger could ever happen.
Why should I be my aunt,
or me, or anyone?
What similarities—
boots, hands, the family voice
I felt in my throat, or even
the *National Geographic*
and those awful hanging breasts—

held us all together
or made us all just one?
How—I didn't know any
word for it—how "unlikely" . . .
How had I come to be here,
like them, and overhear
a cry of pain that could have
got loud and worse but hadn't?

The waiting room was bright
and too hot. It was sliding
beneath a big black wave,
another, and another.

Then I was back in it.
The War was on. Outside,
in Worcester, Massachusetts,
were night and slush and cold,
and it was still the fifth
of February, 1918.

George Herbert

—

LOVE
UNKNOWN

Deare Friend, sit down, the tale is long and sad:
And in my faintings I presume your love
Will more complie then help. A lord I had,
And have, of whom some grounds, which may improve,
I hold for two lives, and both lives in me.
To him I brought a dish of fruit one day,
And in the middle plac'd my heart. But he
                            (I sigh to say)
Lookt on a servant, who did know his eye
Better then you know me, or (which is one)
Then I my self. The servant instantly
Quitting the fruit, seiz'd on my heart alone,
And threw it in a font, wherein did fall
A stream of bloud, which issu'd from the side
Of a great rock: I well remember all,
And have good cause: there it was dipt and dy'd,
And washt, and wrung: the very wringing yet
Enforceth tears. *Your heart was foul, I fear.*
Indeed 'tis true. I did and do commit
Many a fault more than my lease will bear;
Yet still askt pardon, and was not deni'd.
But you shall heare. After my heart was well,
And clean and fair, as I one even-tide
                            (I sigh to tell)
Walkt by my self abroad, I saw a large
And spacious fornace flaming, and thereon
A boyling caldron, round about whose verge
Was in great letters set AFFLICTION.
The greatnesse shew'd the owner. So I went
To fetch a sacrifice out of my fold,
Thinking with that, which I did thus present,
To warm his love, which I did fear grew cold.
But as my heart did tender it, the man,
Who was to take it from me, slipt his hand,
And threw my heart into the scalding pan;
My heart, that brought it (do you understand?)
The offerers heart. *Your heart was hard, I fear.*
Indeed it's true. I found a callous matter

Began to spread and to expatiate there:
But with a richer drug than scalding water
I bath'd it often, ev'n with holy bloud,
Which at a board, while many drunk bare wine,
A friend did steal into my cup for good,
Ev'n taken inwardly, and most divine
To supple hardnesses. But at the length
Out of the caldron getting, soon I fled
Unto my house, where to repair the strength
Which I had lost, I hasted to my bed.
But when I thought to sleep out all these faults
                                        (I sigh to speak)
I found that some had stuff'd the bed with thoughts,
I would say *thorns*. Deare, could my heart not break,
When with my pleasures ev'n my rest was gone?
Full well I understood, who had been there:
For I had giv'n the key to none, but one:
It must be he. *Your heart was dull, I fear.*
Indeed a slack and sleepie state of mind
Did oft possess me, so that when I pray'd,
Though my lips went, my heart did stay behind.
But all my scores were by another paid,
Who took the debt upon him. *Truly, Friend,*
For ought I heare, your Master shows to you
More favour than you wot of. Mark the end.
The Font did onely, what was old, renew:
The Caldron suppled, what was grown too hard:
The Thorns did quicken, what was grown too dull:
All did but strive to mend, what you had marr'd.
Wherefore be cheer'd, and praise him to the full
Each day, each houre, each moment of the week,
Who fain would have you be new, tender, quick.

Comment

A decade ago, when she chose "The Man-Moth" for an anthology, Elizabeth Bishop remarked on the misprint (for "mammoth") by which "an oracle spoke from the page of the *New York Times* . . . One is offered such oracular statements all the time, but often misses them . . . the meaning refuses to stay put." In this recent poem—published since the fortunately mistitled *Complete Poems* —the oracle is, in part, the *National Geographic*, whose "volcano, / black, and full of ashes; / [. . .] spilling over / in rivulets of fire," just like Herbert's "font, wherein did fall / A stream of bloud, which issued from the side / Of a great rock," functions as an instrument of tempering. Pain, war, all the horrors of the flesh, the inadequacies of mere selfhood ("Better than you know me, or (which is one) / Then I my self," Herbert chatters on, as Miss Bishop more laconically discerns: "Without thinking at all / I was my foolish aunt, / I—we—were falling")—these are the means by which we are brought home to ourselves as we must be if we are authentically alive, "new, tender, quick."

Both poems are triumphs of tonality, of patience with material event in its likelihood of revealing what is beyond the material, the image of a speaking voice beguiling us into the deeps until every word (even Bishop's innocuous title, even Herbert's "natural" slip of the tongue: "I found that some had stuff'd the bed with thoughts, / I would say *thorns*") turns incandescent in the "spacious fornace" of experience, of experiment, of trial. The result is that the process I have called tempering (the word covers the famous "temperament" of the modern poet as well as the *Temple* in which the metaphysical one lodges his entire utterance) collocates, fuses: "held us all together / or made us all just one," for to possess an identity is to acknowledge society ("I felt: you are an *I*, / you are an *Elizabeth*, / you are one of *them*."). Such participation is of course explicit in Herbert, for the Sacraments are institutionalized and available, "into my cup for good"; in Bishop, they are momentary and delusive ("the meaning refuses to stay put"), and though at the ultimate source of the word she is a religious poet—religion as a binding together, a unifying of what can never be uniform—there is no redemption for her; there is the *waiting room*, which like the caldron of affliction is "bright and too hot," and "then I was back in it," just as Herbert goes back to bed. "It" is the world, that "scalding pan" which affords these poets their presumption of membership as well as their "sensation of falling."

*John
Malcolm
Brinnin*

SAUL, AFTERWARD, RIDING EAST

[*For Gerald Fitzgerald*]

And as he journeyed, he came near Damascus: and suddenly there shined round about him a light from heaven: / and he fell to the earth, and heard a voice saying unto him, Saul, Saul, why persecutest thou me? / And he said, Who art thou, Lord? And the Lord said, I am Jesus whom thou persecutest . . . / And he trembling and astonished said, Lord, what wilt thou have me to do? And the Lord said unto him, Arise and go into the city, and it shall be told thee what thou must do. / And the men which journeyed with him stood speechless, hearing a voice but seeing no man . . . / And immediately there fell from his eyes as it had been scales: and he received sight forthwith, and arose, and was baptized.

— The Acts of the Apostles, 9:3–18

Still a bit dazed,
I study out the sequence—what
diverting cast of eye,
what random cocking of an ear,
could with such fell abruptness
bounce & so dishevel me? Was it
that fellow in the stinking fleece,
the black figs of his nipples bared,
who watched me drop like a drugged bee?
Those sullen beauties, broad as crabs,
bent to their lettuces & cress? The icy
chuckle of the spring
that rinsed their dragging purples
& vermilions? The two
blue mountains that were always there?

Today is yesterday: my hand,
all by itself, salutes
a door that closes,
or will close.

Hearing a voice (I did hear a voice),
but seeing no man (I saw no man),
I have listened to brass,
accepted any cupful, put on the eunuch's
fastening of silk, rolled over—
a good dog. No wonder
my old road is dark.

Still, the small flowers eat my dust.
Somehow, I wait upon the man I was—

of a commission & a large address,
of rectitude & ample documents.

I think my bones are melting. The reins
keep sliding from my hands.
I jog like a baby, loved.

Courage,
my bruises whisper, you are,
at worst, the subject of a rustic anecdote.
You would not come so far to disappear.
And yet,
this breath that takes my breath away . . .
What wilt thou, Lord, have me to do?

I feel the low sun pushing me to sleep.
Along the walls of these colossal shadows,
light like a rumor runs its fluted scale.
Nothing I see is visible.
Damascus! Damascus!

John Clare

I AM

I am: yet what I am none cares or knows,
    My friends forsake me like a memory lost;
I am the self-consumer of my woes,
    They rise and vanish in oblivious host,
Like shades in love and death's oblivion lost;
And yet I am, and live with shadows tost

Into the nothingness of scorn and noise,
    Into the living sea of waking dreams,
Where there is neither sense of life nor joys,
    But the vast shipwreck of my life's esteems;
And e'en the dearest—that I loved the best—
Are strange—nay, rather stranger than the rest.

I long for scenes where man has never trod,
    A place where woman never smiled or wept;
There to abide with my Creator, God,
    And sleep as I in childhood sweetly slept:
Untroubling and untroubled where I lie,
The grass below—above the vaulted sky.

Comment /

He had been a great success in his twenties, in the delusive guise of "the peasant-poet"; London wearied, love had been a dream, marriage a disaster: dissidence, estrangement, seven children, and not enough to eat. Only poetry survived the evasions into madness and beyond. The last twenty-five years of John Clare's life were spent, or hoarded, in an asylum, unvisited, unrecalled, a Wordsworthian Hölderlin. And in such a place, as a white-haired patriarch of seventy, the human soul that had set out, as a very little boy, on an expedition to find the horizon, the same human soul that had set up, deranged, as a man in his fifties, to be Lord Byron (rich, noble, beloved—known!), wrote this final poem. It is the ultimate assertion of existence, one of the most powerful claims to naked, unpropped identity in the language; the poet, conscious of an exclusion from nature, yearns not for nostalgia's sake but for apocalypse, to be free of nature and of others, to be. . . .

The momentary drollery, then, of reading with this, or even against it, Brinnin's urbane identification—until we are lured by all the false gauds of language into the thing itself, the experience. Saul's? So we are told, though it is Brinnin who wrote, long ago, "I wept for visions, nothing in the world." Then is it Saul or Brinnin who acknowledges the renunciation of "commission & a large address" by the same penetration: "Nothing I see is visible"? Stupefied by the charge, the about-to-be-baptized Saul, "like a baby, loved," is at this moment no more than an identity—not a person, a character, even a mask —nothing but the tenant of existence John Clare celebrates too, the one ecstasy at the outset, the other at the close, beyond pain or joy: "Untroubling and untroubled where I lie, / The grass below—above the vaulted sky."

Robert
Creeley

AIR: CAT BIRD SINGING

Cat bird singing
makes music like sounds coming

at night. The trees, goddamn them,
are huge eyes. They

watch, certainly, what
else should they do? My love

is a person of rare refinement,
and when she speaks,

there is another air,
melody—what Campion spoke of

with his
follow thy fair sunne, unhappie shadow . . .

Catbird, catbird.
O lady hear me. I have no

other
voice left.

Thomas Campion

FOLLOWE THY
FAIRE SUNNE

Followe thy faire sunne, unhappy shadowe,
Though thou be blacke as night,
And she made all of light,
Yet follow thy faire sunne, unhappie shadowe.

Follow her whose light thy light depriveth,
Though here thou liv'st disgrac't,
And she in heaven is plac't,
Yet follow her whose light the world reviveth.

Follow those pure beames whose beautie burneth,
That so have scorched thee,
As thou still blacke must bee,
Til her kind beames thy black to brightnes turneth.

Follow her while yet her glorie shineth:
There comes a luckles night,
That will dim all her light;
And this the black unhappie shade devineth.

Follow still since so thy fates ordained;
The Sunne must have his shade,
Till both at once doe fade,
The Sunne still proud, the shadowe still disdained.

Comment

"I have chiefly aymed to couple my Words and Notes lovingly together," Campion wrote of *his* airs in a preface to the reader; this one, however, has no explicit musical reference in the text itself—the doubleness is all of light and darkness, self and other, source and symbol; and the only, final, unity of the opposed phenomenologies is in extinction—not the doing away with darkness by light (a common conceit of the beloved "killing" the lover), but the end of all things, signaled here by the sudden capitalizing of the real Sun, which is put out along with the shadow, neither one the cause or accompaniment of the other, but both "fading" in the final catastrophe. It is an apocalyptic way of figuring love's constancy, this "luckles night" in which both shadow and sun are dimmed, but it gives us a clue, beyond the affection of Pound and Olson for this musician-poet, why Creeley, in his analogous pang, turns to the conventional lyric—even at a moment when "Campion spoke of" no melody at all, but merely the end of the world, the one thing that can happen only once.

Creeley's music, too, is not explicit, but that of a bird, and the expectation is of course reversed—the cat bird makes music *like* "sounds coming at night," whereas of course it is the bird's sounds coming at night which are like music. Nor *is* it night in this little poem, though the accursed trees are like eyes (so often a nocturnal fancy), and the music, the *other air*, is not the beloved's song but her speech. The poem is about the relegation of analogy, about the moment of overwhelming convergence, when the poet can no longer bear to connect, to relate, to couple words and notes, feelings and phenomena. As always in Creeley, and especially at the verge of declaration, there comes the moment of singleness, of isolated discovery, an apostrophe of separateness as the universe funnels down. It happens at the line "catbird, catbird" (suddenly the word is shoved together, whereas it had been two words, just as Campion's sun becomes the Sun—this is a poetry charged with signs and signals), no more than the constatation of the bird's existence, the music, an energy acknowledged—no more. And then the little tag of convention, "O lady hear me"—the lover's abrupt attempt to impinge on the consciousness of "a person of rare refinement" (the two expressions are ironic in their tone, contrast touchingly with the litle poem's otherwise obdurate colloquialism), and the final aporia—the refusal of just that doubleness Campion invoked by coupling words and notes, sun and shadow, so lovingly together. In Creeley, the ecstasy is one of apocalypse, no longer pairing his voice with the bird's music, as the extraordinary enjambment tells us, but singling out, cutting off reference and relation, discrete, insistently unique, and, in the true sense of the word, incoherent:

> *I have no*

> > *other*
> > *voice left.*

J. V.
Cunningham

MONTANA FIFTY YEARS AGO

Gaunt kept house with her child for the old man,
Met at the train, dust-driven as the sink
She came to, the child white as the alkali.
To the West distant mountains, the Big Lake
to the Northeast. Dead trees and almost dead
In the front yard, the front door locked and nailed,
A handpump in the sink. Outside, a land
Of gophers, cottontails, and rattlesnakes,
In good years of alfalfa, oats, and wheat.
Root cellar, blacksmith shop, milk house, and barn,
Granary, corral. An old *World Almanac*
To thumb at night, the child coughing, the lamp smoked,
The chores done. So he came to her one night,
To the front room, now bedroom, and moved in.
Nothing was said, nothing was ever said.
And then the child died and she disappeared.
This was Montana fifty years ago.

Alexander Pope

ODE ON SOLITUDE

Happy the man, whose wish and care
A few paternal acres bound,
Content to breathe his native air,
     In his own ground.

Whose herds with milk, whose fields with bread,
Whose flocks supply him with attire,
Whose trees in summer yield him shade,
     In winter fire.

Blest! who can unconcern'dly find
Hours, days, and years slide soft away,
In health of body, peace of mind,
     Quiet by day,

Sound sleep by night; study and ease
Together mix'd; sweet recreation,
And innocence, which most does please,
     With meditation.

Thus let me live, unseen, unknown;
Thus unlamented let me dye;
Steal from the world, and not a stone
     Tell where I lye.

Comment /

"For the interesting contrast in ways of life," Mr. Cunningham picks, to put beside his late bleak genre piece "Montana Fifty Years Ago," the earliest Pope poem we have, written before he was twelve, Pope claimed, though the first manuscript of it dates from his twentieth year, when he was writing to Wycherly:

As a man in love with a Mistress, desires no Conversation but hers, so a Man in love with himself, (as most Men are) may be best pleased with his own. . . . We see nothing more commonly, than Men, who for the sake of the circumstantial Part, and meer outside of Life, have been half their Days rambling out of their Nature, and ought to be sent into Solitude to study themselves over again.

Fluent and conventional though this jewel of Pope's juvenilia may be, and merciless though Cunningham's dry decasyllabics certainly sound, the contrast is not so pat, perhaps, between Windsor Forest and our Western fastness as we might first expect. The impulse in Pope which created the grotto at Twickenham, which turned on his pursuers, in the "Epistle to Dr. Arbuthnot," and savagely asked, "What Walls can guard me, or what Shades can hide?"—the impulse to discard and discredit precisely that image of the City by which we so reductively measure him, may be seen even this early, even this ingenuously, to be an effort of subversion, an undermining of civility:

Thus let me live, unseen, unknown;
Thus unlamented let me dye;
Steal from the world, and not a stone
    Tell where I lye.

I wonder how near the surface of consciousness the words "steal" and "lye" were stirring here, suggesting precisely that the monuments are the mendacity, the record the evasion. While the impulse in Cunningham which leads him to name his American Andromache "Gaunt" is nonetheless the affabulative one that tells—however exiguously, however desiccated the decor—a story of passion, sorrow, and inclusive pain. The clue is the *World Almanac*, "thumbed at night," and thereby linking this wordless history to all the rest, to all the contexts which are here set aside; while for all the "flocks" and "fields," the "study" and "ease" of Pope's adolescent ode, the impulse is to crawl away into the cave, the generating dark. "The interesting contrast in ways of life . . ."

James
Dickey

THE SHEEP CHILD

Farm boys wild to couple
With anything   with soft-wooded trees
With mounds of earth   mounds
Of pinestraw   will keep themselves off
Animals by legends of their own:
In the hay-tunnel dark
And dung of barns, they will
Say   I have heard tell

That in a museum in Atlanta
Way back in a corner somewhere
There's this thing that's only half
Sheep   like a woolly baby
Pickled in alcohol   because
Those things can't live   his eyes
Are open   but you can't stand to look
I heard from somebody who . . .

But this is now almost all
Gone. The boys have taken
Their own true wives in the city,
The sheep are safe in the west hill
Pasture   but we who were born there
Still are not sure. Are we,
Because we remember, remembered
In the terrible dust of museums?

Merely with his eyes, the sheep-child may

Be saying   saying

I am here, in my father's house.
I who am half of your world, came deeply

To my mother in the long grass
Of the west pasture, where she stood like moonlight
Listening for foxes. It was something like love
From another world that seized her
From behind, and she gave, not lifting her head
Out of dew, without ever looking, her best
Self to that great need. Turned loose, she dipped her face
Farther into the chill of the earth, and in a sound
Of sobbing   of something stumbling
Away, began, as she must do,
To carry me. I woke, dying,

In the summer sun of the hillside, with my eyes
Far more than human. I saw for a blazing moment
The great grassy world from both sides,
Man and beast in the round of their need,
And the hill wind stirred in my wool,
My hoof and my hand clasped each other,
I ate my one meal
Of milk, and died
Staring. From dark grass I came straight

To my father's house, whose dust
Whirls up in the halls for no reason
When no one comes   piling deep in a hellish mild corner,
And, through my immortal waters,
I meet the sun's grains eye
To eye and they fail at my closet of glass.
Dead, I am most surely living
In the minds of farm boys: I am he who drives
Them like wolves from the hound bitch and calf
And from the chaste ewe in the wind.
They go into woods   into bean fields   they go
Deep into their known right hands. Dreaming of me,
They groan   they wait   they suffer
Themselves, they marry, they raise their kind.

Christopher Smart

from
JUBILATE AGNO

For I will consider my Cat Jeoffrey.
For he is the servant of the Living God, duly and daily serving him.
For at the first glance of the glory of God in the East he worships in his way.
For is this done by wreathing his body seven times round with elegant quickness.
For then he leaps up to catch the musk, which is the blessing of God upon his prayer.
For he rolls upon prank to work it in.
For having done duty and received blessing he begins to consider himself.
For this he performs in ten degrees.
For first he looks upon his fore-paws to see if they are clean.
For secondly he kicks up behind to clear away there.
For thirdly he works it upon stretch with the fore-paws extended.
For fourthly he sharpens his paws by wood.
For fifthly he washes himself.
For sixthly he rolls upon wash.
For seventhly he fleas himself, that he may not be interrupted upon the beat.
For eighthly he rubs himself against a post.
For ninthly he looks up for his instructions.
For tenthly he goes in quest of food.
For having consider'd God and himself he will consider his neighbor.
For if he meets another cat he will kiss her in kindness.
For when he takes his prey he plays with it to give it chance.
For one mouse in seven escapes by his dallying.
For when his day's work is done his business more properly begins.
For [he] keeps the Lord's watch in the night against the adversary.
For he counteracts the powers of darkness by his electrical skin and glaring eyes.

For he counteracts the Devil, who is death, by brisking about the life.

For in his morning orisons he loves the sun and the sun loves him.

For he is of the tribe of Tiger.

For the Cherub Cat is a term of the Angel Tiger.

For he has the subtlety and hissing of a serpent, which in goodness he suppresses.

For he will not do destruction, if he is well-fed, neither will he spit without provocation.

For he purrs in thankfulness, when God tells him he's a good Cat.

For he is an instrument for the children to learn benevolence upon.

For every house is incompleat without him and a blessing is lacking in the spirit.

For the Lord commanded Moses concerning the cats at the departure of the Children of Israel
     from Egypt.

For every family had one cat at least in the bag.

For the English Cats are the best in Europe.

For he is the cleanest in the use of his fore-paws of any quadrupede.

For the dexterity of his defence is an instance of the love of God to him exceedingly.

For he is the quickest to his mark of any creature.

For he is tenacious of his point.

For he is a mixture of gravity and waggery.

For he knows that God is his Saviour.

For there is nothing sweeter than his peace when at rest.

For there is nothing brisker than his life when in motion.

For he is of the Lord's poor and so indeed is he called by benevolence perpetually—
     Poor Jeoffry! poor Jeoffry! the rat has bit thy throat.

For I bless the name of the Lord Jesus that Jeoffry is better.

For the divine spirit comes about his body to sustain it in compleat cat.

For his tongue is exceeding pure so that it has in purity what it wants in musick.

For he is docile and can learn certain things.

For he can set up with gravity which is patience upon approbation.

For he can fetch and carry, which is patience in employment.

For he can jump over a stick which is patience upon proof positive.

For he can spraggle upon waggle at the word of command.

For he can jump from an eminence into his master's bosom.

For he can catch the cork and toss it again.

For he is hated by the hypocrite and miser.

For the former is affraid of detection.

For the latter refuses the charge.

For he camels his back to bear the first notion of business.

For he is good to think on, if a man would express himself neatly.

For he made a great figure in Egypt for his signal services.

For he killed the Icneumon-rat very pernicious by land.

For his ears are so acute that they sting again.

For from this proceeds the passing quickness of his attention.

For by stroaking of him I have found out electricity.

For I perceived God's light about him both wax and fire.

For the Electrical fire is the spiritual substance, which God sends from heaven to sustain the bodies both of man and beast.

For God has blessed him in the variety of his movements.

For, tho he cannot fly, he is an excellent clamberer.

For his motions upon the face of the earth are more than any other quadrupede.

For he can tread to all the measures upon the musick.

For he can swim for life.

For he can creep.

Comment

About the time he published "The Sheep Child," Dickey wrote an essay on Christopher Smart's "Song to David" charged with a kind of incandescent envy, saying, for example, "From the beginning we have suspected the mad of magic and have wanted what they have, the revelations." How practical as well as how exacting those revelations can be is the burden of all magic, and indeed it is a matter of poetry, not merely a manner, to devise the charms and spells, the means of managing the natural for our own ends, whatever the cost to mere reason.

In all of James Dickey's later work there is certainly a Master-of-the-Coven aspect, an erotic aspiration to metamorphosis by which he reconstitutes, in a narrative utterly without ritual, the very mythology or demonism he has been at such pains to disintegrate in his ecstatic meters, his country tropes. No wonder he suspects the mad of magic and covets their presumed revelation —for Dickey there are only terrible blanks, holes in being, where for Smart there is the endless litany, a benediction on the universe inspissated by remarks, some astonishingly practical indeed and some just preposterous, wandering off into the hieratic associationism we call madness, then suddenly jerking back into the neatest observation of feature and detail we call reality, but never for a moment still.

The voice in Smart's *Jubilate Agno* from which this celebrated fragment comes is that gigantic and obsessive prayer which sometimes rises out of literature (and perhaps justifies it), the naming of parts, the saying of sooth, the praising of what may be. It contains the horror of never being able to stop. In Dickey's hot pastoral, the horror is of falling silent, and the voice contains that horror in its strange drops and perforations. Forms are sundered, wrenched apart rather than wrought together; rhythms are an inference from the utterance rather than a condition of it; lines are spread or sprung to produce luminous, layered walls of print, cunningly enjambed or rifted round great white holes.

Dickey cannot apostrophize his sheep child as Smart, in his litaneutical peace, praises Jeoffrey; his is the imagination of metamorphosis, and he must *become* what the madman addresses, and out of that rapture of the impossible and the visionary wrest his speculation about the likelihood of mustering the animal resources, the natural powers with the human, giving us, as he says again of Smart, "what we have always wanted from the insane: the life-extending, life-deepening insight, the ultimate symbolic sanity."

Alan
Dugan

FROM ROME.
FOR MORE PUBLIC FOUNTAINS IN NEW YORK CITY

Oh effervescent palisades of ferns in drippage,
the air sounds green by civic watered bronze
fountains in New York City. Hierarchs of spray
go up and down in office: they scour the noons
when hot air stinks to itself from Jersey's smoke
and the city makes itself a desert of cement.
Moses! Command the sun to august temperance!
When water rises freely over force and poises,
cleaning itself in the dirty air, it falls back
on the dolphins, Poseidon, and moss-headed nymphs,
clean with the dirt of air left cleansed by its
clear falling, and runs down cooly with the heat
to its commune, pooling. What public utility!
The city that has working fountains, that lights
them up at night electrically, that does not say
to thirsters at its fountains: DO NOT DRINK!—
that city is well ordered in its waters and drains
and dresses its corruption up in rainbows, false
to the eye but how expressive of a cool truth being.
The unitary water separates, novel on its heights,
and falls back to its unity, discoursing. So let
New York City fountains be the archives of ascent
that teach the low high styles in the open air
and frondage of event! Then all our subway selves
could learn to fall with grace, after sparkling,
and the city's life acknowledge the water of life.

Jonathan Swift

—

A
DESCRIPTION
OF THE
MORNING

Now hardly here and there a hackney-coach
Appearing showed the ruddy morn's approach.
Now Betty from her master's bed had flown,
And softly stole to discompose her own;
The slipshod 'prentice from his master's door
Had pared the dirt and sprinkled around the floor.
Now Moll had whirled her mop with dexterous airs,
Prepared to scrub the entry and the stairs.
The youth with broomy stumps began to trace
The kennel-edge, where wheels had worn the place.
The small-coal man was heard with cadence deep,
Till drowned in shriller notes of chimney-sweep:
Duns at his lordship's gate began to meet;
And brickdust Moll had screamed through half the street.
The turnkey now his flock returning sees,
Duly let out a-nights to steal for fees:
The watchful bailiffs take their silent stands,
And schoolboys lag with satchels in their hands.

Comment /

Urbanity is a tough virtue—or else it is no more than an easy vice: the capacity to order a good dinner or make a good after-dinner speech, when what is needed is the conscience of the *agape* between.

Disabused, gingerly, and without trust, Dugan has the authentic tonality of the urbane: "I shall walk out bravely into the daily accident." This is stoicism bordering on paranoia, of course, a poetry of *passing sentence*, "walled away from wilderness / by absence in stone and iron," as Dugan says of his animals in the zoo. Like Swift's anti-pastoral, Dugan's urban eclogue is a nostalgia for a language, a resentful yearning expressed as satire, as the criticism of *this* reality in terms of *that* convention. Swift's Putney counterparts of pastoral are, as Martin Price has noted, term-for-term indeed: instead of Aurora leaving Tithonus's bed, we have "Betty from her master's bed"; instead of the innocent shepherd, we have the corrupt jailer; instead of gentle showers, we have apprentices sprinkling shop floors; instead of breezes, we have the whirling mop; instead of singing birds, we have the "shriller notes of chimney-sweep."

Like the eighteenth-century poem, the twentieth-century one, which substitutes Rome for pastoral, and offsets broken imperium by democratic degradation, is nourished by a discovery —the discovery that there *is* another language, a language appropriate to selfhood, to private experience, personal ecstasy, and personal loss, but that this language is in the public language. Within the official received version ("the city makes itself a desert of cement"), there is the shrinking secret which is life's, yet which must be recorded in the terms of the standard and the state. Hence the games, the playfulness, the wit ("let / New York City fountains be the archives of ascent / that teach the low high styles in the open air"), the devices and contrivances to outwit language, to trick utterance into revealing the truth it shrouds.

To speak at all means to speak for others, which is why Dugan takes his example and his text from the great public works of "corruption," from Roman fountains—in order to institute, back home, the significant pluralism of water:

> *Then all our subway selves*
> *could learn to fall with grace, after sparkling,*
> *and the city's life acknowledge the water of life.*

It was Swift's practice, we are told, to have two of his men-servants brought in to listen to his poems being read, "which, if they did not comprehend, he would alter and amend, until they understood it perfectly well, and then would say, *This will do, for I write to the vulgar, more than to the learned.*" I can conceive Dugan's incredulous grin at the notion of "two of his men-servants," but there is an astonishing congruity here—the shared sense of "public utility," the persuasion that the poet is the conscience of his city—urbane, indeed:

> *The unitary water separates, novel on its heights,*
> *and falls back to unity, discoursing.*

That is the entire justice of urbanity, that is the *ars poetica* of a citizen who knows that the private life signifies only within the public one, the noumenal only within the phenomenal.

Irving
Feldman

MY OLSON ELEGY

I set out now
in a box upon the sea.   —Maximus VI

Three weeks, and now I hear!
What a headstart for the other elegists!
I say, No matter! by any route and manner
we shall arrive beside you together.
Envy, Triumph, Pride, Derision:
such passionate oarsmen drive my harpooner,
he hurls himself through your side.
You lie and wait to be overtaken.
You absent yourself at every touch.

It was an adolescent, a poetboy,
who told me—one of that species, spoiled,
self-showing, noisy, conceited, *épatants*—
voice breaking from the ego-distance like
a telephone's, not a voice indeed
but one in facsimile, recon-
stituted static, a locust voice,
exhumed, resurrected, chirring
in its seventeenth year, contentedly
saying, "And I've just completed
section fifteen of my Olson elegy."

Landscape on legs, old Niagara!—all
the unique force, the common vacancy,

the silence and seaward tumultuous gorge
slowly clogging with your own *disjecta*,
tourists, trivia, history,
disciples, picnickers in hell;
oh great Derivative! in quest
of your unknown author, the source
—a flying bit of the beginning blast,
a sky-shard where early thunder slumbers:
the first syllabic grunt, a danger,
a nameless name, a tap on the head; you,
Olson!, whale, thrasher, bard of bigthink,
your cargo of ambergris and pain,
your steamy stupendous sputtering
—all apocalypse and no end:
precocious larvae have begun to try
the collected works beneath your battered sides.

See them now! dazzling elegists sitting
on their silvery kites on air
like symbols in flight, swooping daredevils
jockey for position, mount a hasty breeze
and come careering at your vastness
to read among the gulls and plover
—but the natural cries of birds do not

console us for our gift of speech.
Embarrassed before the sea and silence
we do not rise or sing,
wherefore this choir of eternal boys
strut and sigh and puff their chests and stare
outward from the foundering beach.

King of the flowering deathboat, falls,
island, leviathan, starship night,
you plunge to the primitive deep
where satire's puny dreadful monsters,
its Follies and its Vices, cannot reach,
and swim among their lost originals
—free, forgotten, powerful, moving
wholly in a universe of rhythm—
and re-enter your own first Fool,

inventing happiness out of nothing.
You are the legend death and the sea have seized
in order to become explicable.

—Smell of salt is everywhere,
speed and space burn monstrousness
away, exaltation blooms in the clear:
fair weather, great *bonanza*, the high!,
swelling treasure, blue catch of heaven.
The swimmer like the sea reaches every shore.
Superlative song levitates from lips
of the glowing memorialists,
their selves flash upward in the sun.

Now you are heavier than earth, everything
has become lighter than the air.

John Milton

—

from
LYCIDAS

. . . Ay me! whilst thee the shores and sounding
     seas
Wash far away, where'er thy bones are hurled;
Whether beyond the stormy Hebrides,
Where thou perhaps under the whelming tide
Visit'st the bottom of the monstrous world;
Or whether thou, to our moist vows denied,
Sleep'st by the fable of Bellerus old,
Where the great Vision of the guarded mount
Looks toward Namancos and Bayona's hold.
Look homeward, Angel, now, and melt with
     ruth:
And, O ye dolphins, waft the hapless youth.
   Weep no more, woeful shepherds, weep
     no more,
For Lycidas, your sorrow, is not dead,
Sunk though he be beneath the watery floor,
So sinks the day-star in the ocean bed,
And yet anon repairs his drooping head,
And tricks his beams, and with new-spangled
     ore
Flames in the forehead of the morning sky:
So Lycidas sunk low, but mounted high,
Through the dear might of him that walked
     the waves,

Where, other groves and other streams along,
With nectar pure his oozy locks he laves,
And hears the unexpressive nuptial song,
In the blest kingdoms meek of joy and love.
There entertain him all the Saints above,
In solemn troops, and sweet societies,
That sing, and singing in their glory move,
And wipe the tears for ever from his eyes.
Now, Lycidas, the shepherds weep no more;
Henceforth thou art the Genius of the shore,
In thy large recompense, and shalt be good
To all that wander in that perilous flood.

   Thus sang the uncouth swain to th'oaks
     and rills,
While the still morn went out with sandals
     grey;
He touched the tender stops of various quills,
With eager thought warbling his Doric lay;
And now the sun had stretched out all the
     hills,
And now was dropped into the western bay;
At last he rose, and twitched his mantle blue;
To-morrow to fresh woods, and pastures new.

Comment /

We may entertain, on the evidence provided—the enormity of Charles Olson in both accomplishment and conduct; the insignificance of Edward King as a person, a poet—the same doubts about Feldman's relation to "Maximus" that we debate, still, about Milton's to "Lycidas." The insistent possessiveness of the new elegy's very title suggests at once the kind of organized violence (and what else is poetry?) being done to a great tradition, acknowledged here as great and gradually operative in the enterprise of mourning: at the end a means of releasing the elegist into his own powers, his own primacy. The effort in both poems, then, will be to discriminate a poet's—the speaking poet's—source from his resources, first and last, to enact, to dramatize his resolve—in the face of competition, outrage, blunders—to release what is individual from the thrall of what is merely personal (heretical), to dissolve irrelevance and thereby solve the disputed relation between life and death, poetry and permanence.

It will be the converse of his overwhelming predecessor's tactic which Feldman undertakes. Whereas Milton's hidden god was salvaged from the deeps before he had achieved his identity among us as anything more than a drowned shepherd, Feldman's notorious old poet is revealed in his sacred or sanctifying role only when he has been identified with—immersed in —the destructive, transforming element:

You are the legend death and the sea have seized in order to become explicable.

The substance of things grieved for in *Lycidas* is grandly rejoiced over, celebrated in Feldman's exultant elegy for his monster predecessor (*monster* = something shown, *demonstrated*); moreover, the drowned secrets which in Milton are redeemed ("Henceforth thou art the Genius of the shore, / In thy large recompense, and shalt be good / To all that wander") are precisely the ones which must *remain* drowned to be functional and forgiving ("free, forgotten, powerful, moving / wholly in a universe of rhythm— / [. . .] inventing happiness out of nothing"). Only submerged can a poet "console us for our gift of speech."

Astonishing in its decorum, a recuperation of baroque diction (it is his finest poem so far, and the source of the ominous title of his fourth book, *lost originals*), Feldman's elegy asserts its actuality not by any surrender of magniloquence, not by a modish shrinking from "superlative song," but by its reversal of conduct: whereas the movement of "Lycidas" is from despair through a series of insights to triumphant joy, that of "My Olson Elegy" is from *ressentiment* through a series of submissions to a dispersed, dispensing illumination: death becomes an acceptance of earth (and water) so enormous that what had appeared to be an immortal triumph of poetry turns out merely another action of mortality, and that is the true triumph—Adonis recycled. "The swimmer like the sea reaches every shore."

70

Edward
Field

MY POLISH GRANDMA

Grandma and the children left at night.
It was forbidden to go. In those days
the Czar and his cossacks rode through the town at whim
killing Jews and setting fire to straw roofs
while just down the road the local Poles
sat laughing as they drank liquor.

Grandpa had gone to America first
and earned the money for the rest of the family to come over.
So they left finally, the whole brood of them
with the hired agent running the show,
an impatient man, and there were so many kids
and the bundles kept falling apart
and poor grandma was frightened of him.

She gave the man all the money
but she couldn't round up the kids fast enough for him.
They were children after all and didn't understand
and she was so stupid and clumsy herself,
carrying food for all of them and their clothes
and could she leave behind her pots?
Her legs hurt already; they were always swollen
from the hard work, the childbearing, and the cold.

They caught the train and there was a terrible moment
when the conductor came by for the tickets:
The children mustn't speak or he would know they were Jewish,
they had no permits to travel—Jews weren't allowed.
But the agent knew how to handle it,
everybody got *shmeared*, that means money got you everywhere.

The border was the worst. They had to sneak across at night.
The children mustn't make a sound, not even the babies.
Momma was six and she didn't want to do anything wrong
but she wasn't sure what to do.
The man led them through the woods
and beyond they could hear dogs barking from the sentry hut,
and then they had to run all of them down the ravine to the other side,
grandma broken down from childbearing with her bundles
and bad legs and a baby in her arms,
they ran all the children across the border
or the guards might shoot them
and if the little ones cried, the agent said he would smother them.

They got to a port finally.
Grandpa had arranged for cabin passage, not steerage,
but the agent cheated and put them in the hold
so they were on the low deck looking up at the rich people.
My momma told me how grandma took care of all her children,
how Jake didn't move anymore he was so seasick, maybe even dead,
and if people thought he was dead
they would throw him overboard like garbage, so she hid him.
The rich tossed down oranges to the poor children—
my momma had never had one before.

They came to New York, to the tenements,
a fearful new place, a city, country people in the city.
My momma, who had been roly-poly in slow Poland,
got skinny and pimply in zippy New York.
Everybody grew up in a new way.
And now my grandma is dead and my momma is old
and we her children are all scattered over the earth
speaking a different language and forgetting
why it was so important
to go to a new country.

Tu Fu

—

THE ROAD TO PENGYA

How well I remember those days of danger
    and hardship,
fleeing northward:
                Night near Pengya
with a clear moon painting hill and stream
a brilliant white; on the road
our whole family walking,
ashamed to meet anyone
because of our pitiful condition;
the cry of birds echoing through valleys.
No one was going in the direction
we were coming from.

My tiny girl baby, hungry, kept biting me and
                screaming,
and fearing wild animals would attack us,
I covered her mouth to stop the noise
which only made her scream more;
but my little boy was old enough to
                understand
and searched for bitter wild berries to eat.

For the ten days we travelled on that route, it
                poured
and with nothing to protect us from the rain
we held on to each other shivering

as we waded through deep mud, at times
walking all day but only covering a few miles,
living off the land, sleeping under trees.
Each day as we set out, everything was wet;
sunset when we stopped, the air was heavy
              with mist.

After resting awhile at Chouchiawa
we went through Lutse Pass
to the home of my friend Sun, a former judge,
who out of pity opened his door to us,
lit a lamp, brought water to wash my feet,
made paper cutouts to cheer us up,
then called his wife and children to welcome
              us—
they cried as they heard our terrible story.
My children had already fallen asleep
when my friend awakened them with food.

Then, saying we were brothers,
he moved his things out, giving us his room,
and invited us to live with him,
promising that whatever we needed he would
              get for us.
In a time of trouble
you need a friend like Sun.

Once we were together, my friend and I,
then life parted us.
Tribesmen were fighting us then, and they
              still are.
How I'd like to have wings
and fly back to him.

—Adapted by Edward Field
from the translation by Rewi Alley

Comment /

Not Cavafy, after all, not Auden or Whitman as he has elsewhere invoked them in speaking of his two wry, yearning books—books not so much of poems as of spiels, recitals, routines, "selected short subjects," the caption under which "My Polish Grandma" rejects its address, or addresses its rejection—but the altogether unmistakable (because mistaken, translated, *other*) plainsong of late T'ang lamentation stands behind or beside that mysterious tonality of Edward Field's poetry: a poetry without meter, rhyme, image, without the diet of disciplines and strictures we think of as constituting that shaped share of literature required by *verse*. It is something more than inscrutable, merely, the fact that we can tell that this *is* poetry, that it becomes so, in Field's case as in Tu Fu's, by articulating an impulse which usually begins before "literature" or vibrates in our minds long after we have put down the book, the impulse to testify, to bear witness to the truth. More than inscrutable because it is heretical: rejecting metaphor, Field (like Tu Fu, at least like Tu Fu in translation, certainly a disoriented version) resorts to metonymy, the shift from one sign to another within the same meaning—a procedure, as Roman Jakobson points out, which is at the origin of all the arts of narrative. Field's poems, then, will be telling ones, the stories of a voice in certain defective or defeated circumstances (there is no narrative in heaven; the recording angel is a fallen one).

Whereas Tu Fu's is the bitterness of failure and exile in a ruined empire, Field's is, of course, the bitterness of failure and exile in a rich and outrageous republic: yet the cost to individual lives, to private persons (who else, Field would ask, undertakes to write poems?), is the same, and the accounting of such costs constitutes the poem here. Only a language so entirely lacking in negativity, a diction so submissive to the arbitrary, *could* account for these disasters—here not even the tension engendered by enjambment is tolerable; each line must tell its own tale, shunted back to the left-hand margin only once it has run itself out, never shored up by that other energy of a constant rhythm of expectations which is verse. In Field as in the apparently natural phrasing of the Chinese master (could anything be natural which seems so natural as all that?), there will be in evidence none of the pressures and pains of manipulation: the poem is not fingered or even handled, certainly it is unarmed—merely embodied, by the speaking voice. Language is reduced—or is it enlarged?—to its exclusively metonymic function: one damned thing after another, rather than one thing replacing another (the latter is always an effort suggesting redemption, transcendence, metaphor as Assumption), until only the poem entire is an image—of itself. "Only a suffering people have any virtue," Edward Field remarks in one of his "Variety Photoplays," and he affords the suffering as he enforces the virtue here, under the sign of his great Eastern forbear (or forbearance), the character of telling . . . telling the truth.

Donald Finkel

THE CROSS-EYED LOVER

[*for C*]

1

I have a friend, she says.
I watch the silver minnow
swimming in the shadow
that flows between her breasts,
caught on a silver string.
There is a smile on her face,
I know without looking.

2

Homer went blind,
Milton went blind, looking,
Justice went blind, looking too long at Reason;
Van Gogh sent the Muse
his ear, as a token,
if only he could keep on looking.
(She hung the sun between
her burning yellow breasts;
fried to a golden brown
the brain behind his eyes,
bright blue to the end
and clear as glass.)

3

Cupid tied the bandage on himself.
Under a layer of linen
a forty-six-year-old beautician from De-troit
offers just as sweet a
target as Brigitte.
Only hanged men and little kids
learn quickly enough how not to look through it.

4

I have a friend myself.
All day he peers at naked wenches
sprawling on red velvet couches
or artificial grass,
upside-down on five-by-seven inches
of ground glass.
He says it is an art. (I have an art myself.)

5

Fuad the fakir stares at the sun all day,
all day he turns his whiskered puss to the sun;
he knows damned well his eyes
were burned out years ago.
And what do you think he does
after the sun goes down?
Wouldn't you give your shell-like ear to know.

6

My friend Fuad.
My pal Milton.
Meet my wife, the Muse.
(A silver mermaid leaps between her breasts;
I know without looking.)
Only a brassière salesman in his blue suède
                    shoes
could look on her face, long,
and not go blind.

John Keats

—

LA BELLE DAME SANS MERCI

Ah, what can ail thee, knight-at-arms,
    Alone and palely loitering?
The sedge has wither'd from the lake,
    And no birds sing.

Ah, what can ail thee, knight-at-arms,
    So haggard and so woe-begone?
The squirrel's granary is full,
    And the harvest's done.

I see a lily on thy brow
    With anguish moist and fever dew
And on thy cheeks a fading rose
    Fast withereth too.

I met a lady in the meads,
    Full beautiful—a faery's child,
Her hair was long, her foot was light,
    And her eyes were wild.

I made a garland for her head,
    And bracelets too, and fragrant zone;
She look'd at me as she did love,
    And made sweet moan.

I set her on my pacing steed,
    And nothing else saw all day long,
For sidelong she would bend, and sing
    A faery's song.

She found me roots of relish sweet,
    And honey wild, and manna dew,
And sure in language strange she said,
    "I love thee true."

She took me to her elfin grot,
    And there she wept, and sigh'd full sore,
And there I shut her wild wild eyes
    With kisses four.

And there she lullèd me asleep
    And there I dream'd—Ah! woe betide!
The latest dream I ever dream'd
    On the cold hill side.

I saw pale kings, and princes too,
    Pale warriors, death-pale were they all;
They cried—"La belle Dame sans Merci
    Hath thee in thrall!"

I saw their starved lips in the gloam
    With horrid warning gapèd wide,
And I awoke and found me here
    On the cold hill side.

And this is why I sojourn here
    Alone and palely loitering,
Though the sedge is wither'd from the lake,
    And no birds sing.

Comment |

"Where is your Self to be found? Always in the deepest enchantment you have experienced." Of course, like all such truth, like all true aphorisms, Hofmannsthal's is susceptible of reversal, proved by the mirror. That is where the self is to be *lost*, too—in the deepest enchantments of experience: for Keats as for Finkel, in nature, song, and love. Nor is it much of a paradox that such losing is finding, when we remember that finding is, at the root, *inventing*, making what might never have been there at all yet what—if we go about losing rightly: "I have an art myself" the right assumption—cannot be other than what it is. Which is why poetry is anything and everything *but* self-expression, being rather, as Keats says, "richer entanglements, enthralments far / More self-destroying." The knight-at-arms is bereft, his world has withered, and he is yielded up, according to Keats, to "his future doom, which is but to awake." In like case, the cross-eyed lover takes Keats's "journey homeward to habitual self," traveling out of blind ecstasy—blind from too much looking—and into the toils of an averted life, a waking prose.

Few birds sing in the suburbs—"my wife, the Muse" is an intermittent affair by her very constancy, the converse of faery for the modern lover who is not blind or even palely loitering, but cross-eyed (if you keep doing that, as we were always told, they'll stay that way for good; for the better, Finkel insinuates), suffering the occasional mutilations of his fate but cunning enough to evade them as well ("I know without looking"). Indeed, it is the great lineage of nympholepts, from Thomas the Rhymer through this haggard knight to Humbert Humbert which constitutes the cross-eyed lover's lore: *they* are what he knows, they afford him a certain release, a momentary erosion of the spell, as we can discern in his broken rhythms, his off-hand associations, his anti-poetry: "my pal Milton," "a brassière salesman in his blue suède shoes"). Where Keats defends "kisses four" in the name of decorum ("Why four kisses—you will say—why four? because I wish to restrain the headlong impetuosity of my Muse—she would have fain said 'score' without hurting the rhyme—but we must temper the Imagination as the Critics say with Judgment"), Finkel defers to insolence in the name of deformity ("Wouldn't you give your shell-like ear to know"); the modern poet's hand-to-mouth music, his determined grimaces of allusion and tone are desperate measures to keep out of the ecstatic center, to avoid looking when seeing is blindness, when finders are losers, as well as an acknowledgment of that other absorption, that deepest enchantment inside the blindfold, under the bandage, in the dark.

*Allen
Ginsberg*

WALES VISITATION

White fog lifting & falling on mountain-brow
      Trees moving in rivers of wind
                        The clouds arise
    as on a wave, gigantic eddy lifting mist
      above teeming ferns exquisitely swayed
                      along a green crag
    glimpsed thru mullioned glass in valley raine—

Bardic, O Self, Visitacione, tell naught
    but what seen by one man in a vale in Albion,
      of the folk, whose physical sciences end in Ecology,
           the wisdom of earthly relations,
      of mouths & eyes interknit ten centuries visible
          orchards of mind language manifest human,
    of the satanic thistle that raises its horned symmetry
      flowering above sister grass-daisies' pink tiny
           bloomlets angelic as lightbulbs—

Remember 160 miles from London's symmetrical thorned tower
    & network of TV pictures flashing bearded your Self
  the lambs on the tree-nooked hillside this day bleating
  heard in Blake's old ear, & the silent thought of Wordsworth in eld Stillness
  clouds passing through skeleton arches of Tintern Abbey—
        Bard Nameless as the Vast, babble to Vastness!

All the Valley quivered, one extended motion, wind
        undulating on mossy hills
  a giant wash that sank white fog delicately down red runnels
        on the mountainside
  whose leaf-branch tendrils moved asway
        in granitic undertow down—

and lifted the floating Nebulus upward, and lifted the arms of the trees
      and lifted the grasses an instant in balance
          and lifted the lambs to hold still
     and lifted the green of the hill, in one solemn wave

A solid mass of Heaven, mist-infused, ebbs thru the vale,
    a wavelet of Immensity, lapping gigantic through Llanthony Valley,
     the length of all England, valley upon valley under Heaven's ocean
                      tonned with cloud-hang,
         Heaven balanced on a grassblade—
Roar of the mountain wind slow, sigh of the body,
     One Being on the mountainside stirring gently
        Exquisite scales trembling everywhere in balance,
one motion thru the cloudy sky-floor shifting on the million feet of daisies,
one Majesty the motion that stirred wet grass quivering
     to the farthest tendril of white fog poured down
         through shivering flowers on the mountain's head—

No imperfection in the budded mountain,
    Valleys breathe, heaven and earth move together,
   daisies push inches of yellow air, vegetables tremble,
       green atoms shimmer in grassy mandalas,
sheep speckle the mountainside, revolving their jaws with empty eyes,
         horses dance in the warm rain,
    tree-lined canals network through live farmland,
         blueberries fringe stone walls
     on hill breasts nippled with hawthorn,
peasants croak up meadow-bellies haired with fern—

Out, out on the hillside, into the ocean sound, into delicate gusts of wet air,
Fall on the ground, O great Wetness, O Mother, No harm on thy body!
Stare close, no imperfection in the grass,
      each flower Buddha-eye, repeating the story,
        the myriad-formed soul
Kneel before the foxglove raising green buds, mauve bells drooped
    doubled down the stem trembling antennae,
   & look in the eyes of the branded lambs that stare
    breathing stockstill under dripping hawthorn—

I lay down mixing my beard with the wet hair of the mountainside,
       smelling the brown vagina-moist ground, harmless,
              tasting the violet thistle-hair, sweetness—
One being so balanced, so vast, that its softest breath
       moves every floweret in the stillness on the valley floor,
       trembles lamb-hair hung gossamer rain-beaded in the grass,
lifts trees on their roots, birds in the great draught
       hiding their strength in the rain, bearing same weight,

Groan thru breast and neck, a great Oh! to earth heart
                     Calling our Presence together
       The great secret is no secret
              Senses fit the winds,
                     Visible is visible,
       rain-mist curtains wave through the bearded vale,
              grey atoms wet the wind's Kaballah
Crosslegged on a rock in dusk rain,
       rubber-booted in soft grass, mind moveless,
       breath trembles in white daisies by the roadside,
              Heaven breath and my own symmetric
       Airs wavering thru antlered green fern
drawn in my navel, same breath as breathes thru Capel-Y-Ffn,
       Sounds of Aleph and Aum
                     through forests of gristle,
       my skull and Lord Hereford's Knob equal,
                     All Albion one.

What did I notice? Particulars! The
       vision of the great One is myriad—
smoke curls upward from ash tray,
              house fire burned low,
The night, still wet & moody black heaven
                     starless
       upward in motion with wet wind.

                     July 29, 1967 (LSD)—August 3, 1967 (London)

William Wordsworth

—

from

ODE: INTIMATIONS OF IMMOR-
TALITY FROM RECOLLECTIONS
OF EARLY CHILDHOOD

III

Now, while the birds thus sing a joyous song,
 And while the young lambs bound
  As to the tabor's sound,
To me alone there came a thought of grief:
A timely utterance gave that thought relief,
 And I again am strong:
The cataracts blow their trumpets from the
  steep;
No more shall grief of mine the season wrong;
I hear the Echoes through the mountains
  throng,
The winds come to me from the fields of sleep,
 And all the earth is gay;
  Land and sea
 Give themselves up to jollity,
  And with the heart of May
Doth every Beast keep holiday;—
  Thou Child of Joy,
Shout round me, let me hear thy shouts, thou
  happy Shepherd-boy!

IV

Ye blessèd Creatures, I have heard the call
 Ye to each other make; I see
The heavens laugh with you in your jubilee;
 My heart is at your festival,
 My head has its coronal,
The fulness of your bliss, I feel—I feel it all.
 Oh evil day! if I were sullen
 While Earth herself is adorning
  This sweet May-morning,
 And the Children are culling
  On every side,
In a thousand valleys far and wide,
Fresh flowers; while the sun shines
  warm,
And the Babe leaps up on his Mother's arm:—
 I hear, I hear, with Joy I hear!
 —But there's a Tree, of many, one,
A single Field which I have looked upon,
Both of them speak of something that is gone:
 The Pansy at my feet
 Doth the same tale repeat:
Whither is fled the visionary gleam?
Where is it now, the glory and the dream?

V

Our birth is but a sleep and a forgetting:
The soul that rises with us, our life's Star,
 Hath had elsewhere its setting,
  And cometh from Afar:
Not in entire forgetfulness

And not in utter nakedness,
But trailing clouds of glory do we come
   From God, who is our home:
Heaven lies about us in our infancy!
Shades of the prison-house begin to close
   Upon the growing Boy
But he beholds the light, and whence it flows,
   He sees it in his joy;
The Youth who daily farther from the east
    Must travel, still is Nature's Priest,
    And by the vision splendid
    Is on his way attended;
At length the Man perceives it die away
And fade into the light of common day.

      IX
   O joy! that in our embers
   Is something that doth live,
   That nature yet remembers
   What was so fugitive!
The thought of our past years in me doth
     breed
Perpetual benediction: not indeed
For that which is most worthy to be blest;
Delight and liberty, the simple creed
Of Childhood, whether busy or at rest,
With new-fledged hope still fluttering in his
     breast:—
    Not for these I raise
    The song of thanks and praise;

But for those obstinate questionings
Of sense and outward things,
   Fallings from us, vanishings;
   Blank misgivings of a Creature
Moving about in worlds not realised,
High instincts before which our mortal
     Nature
Did tremble like a guilty Thing surprised:
    But for those first affections,
    Those shadowy recollections
   Which, be they what they may,
Are yet the fountain-light of all our day,
Are yet a master-light of all our seeing;
    Uphold us, cherish, and have power to
     make
Our noisy years seem moments in the being
Of the eternal Silence: truths that wake
    To perish never:
Which neither listlessness, nor mad
     endeavour,
    Nor man nor Boy,
Nor all that is at enmity with joy,
Can utterly abolish or destroy!
    Hence in a season of calm weather
    Though inland far we be
Our Souls have sight of that immortal sea
    Which brought us hither,
    Can in a moment travel thither,
And see the Children sport upon the shore,
And hear the mighty waters rolling evermore.

Comment /

He visited Wales, then, fresh or stale from a television stint, from London's replications of himself (for Allen Ginsberg is, however solitary, a frowning public man by now, a prophet who comes down from his hills and in the marketplace shakes his fist, even as his tambourine); he came primed and seconded with the intervals of poetic forbears—of the great modern Welshman who, in his culminating apprehension of himself as earth's heir, in "Fern Hill," "sang in my chains like the sea"; of Blake, long caught in his unstopped ear, who echoes here, there, and everywhere in this poem, as in a line like "Heaven balanced on a grassblade," for indeed Allen Ginsberg came to Wales to announce such auguries of innocence as that "The Bleat, Bark, Bellow and Roar / Are Waves that Beat on Heaven's Shore"; and most tellingly, of Whitman, the greatest sea-singer of his country (though Allen Ginsburg would have said, of course, "I am the man, *I rejoiced*, I was there"). And with these great visionary identifications upon him, he came as well with the oceanic assumptions, as Freud calls them, of lysergic acid, in order to write in Wales the great eclogue of our decade, the poem "of mouths and eyes interknit" which, like the Wordsworth ode it aspires to, gains "sight of that immortal sea / Which brought us hither," where with Blake and Whitman and Thomas, Ginsberg too can "see the Children sport upon the shore / And hear the mighty waters rolling evermore."

It is all in the seeing and hearing, in the exactitude of accommodation between the senses and the cosmos, so delicately suited that the lineaments of the apocalyptic giant are able to be united at the climax of Ginsberg's submission to what he sees and hears:

Sounds of Aleph and Aum
through forests of gristle,
my skull and Lord Hereford's Knob equal,
All Albion one.

On the Welsh hilltop, Hebrew and Hindu wisdoms meet, the poet and the landscape materialize each other in "forests of gristle," and Albion is one—again. "What did I notice?" Ginsberg asks in his beautiful epilogue, and with Blake answers, "Particulars!" Indeed, along with his choice, he sends along this cheerful account of the endeavor:

Promethean text recollected in emotion revised in tranquility continuing tradition of ancient nature language mediates between psychedelic inspiration and humane ecology and integrates acid classic Unitive Vision with democratic eyeball particulars . . .

Surely that is so, yet it will not serve to account for the poem's success, the kind of success gained in its great fourth stanza, beginning "All the Valley quivered" and ending, though the sentence flows on, "and lifted the green of the hill, in one solemn wave." Here the gift, like Wordsworth's, is the talent for uniting the heard and the seen in the one knowledge—as another poet says, so that the ear can crawl back into the eye; it is, this talent, the capacity the mind has to keep the sentence rising, five times "lifting" the elements into the "sigh of the body, / One Being on the mountainside stirring gently." It is not acid or ancestors which can account for the splendor of this poem, then—it is the trust in the eye's particular and the ear's perception, the movement of the mind which makes sense only when the senses make it:

The night, still wet & moody black heaven
starless
upward in motion with wet wind.

Anthony
Hecht

THE VOW

In the third month, a sudden flow of blood,
The mirth of tabrets ceaseth, and the joy
Also of the harp. The frail image of God
Lay spilled and formless. Neither girl nor boy,
But yet blood of my blood, nearly my child.
                All that long day
Her pale face turned to the window's mild
                Featureless grey.

And for some nights she whimpered as she dreamed
The dead thing spoke, saying: "Do not recall
Pleasure at my conception. I am redeemed
From pain and sorrow. Mourn rather for all
Who breathlessly issue from the bone gates,
                The gates of horn,
For truly it is best of all the fates
                Not to be born.

"Mother, a child lay gasping for bare breath
On Christmas Eve when Santa Claus had set
Death in the stocking, and the lights of death
Flamed in the tree. O, if you can, forget
You were the child, turn to my father's lips
                Against the time
When his cold hand puts forth its fingertips
                Of jointed lime."

Doctors of Science, what is man that he
Should hope to come to a good end? *The best
Is not to have been born.* And could it be
That Jewish diligence and Irish jest
The consent of flesh and a midwinter storm
                Had reconciled,
Was yet too bold a mixture to inform
                A simple child?

Even as gold is tried, Gentile and Jew.
If that ghost was a girl's, I swear to it:
Your mother shall be far more blessed than you.
And if a boy's, I swear: The flames are lit
That shall refine us; they shall not destroy
                A living hair.
Your younger brothers shall confirm in joy
                This that I swear.

William
Shakespeare

—

KING LEAR
Act IV, Scene VII

CORDELIA
How does my royal lord? How fares your Majesty?

LEAR
You do me wrong to take me out o' the grave,
Thou art a soul in bliss; but I am bound
Upon a wheel of fire, that mine own tears
Do scald like molten lead.

CORDELIA

Sir, do you know me?

LEAR
You are a spirit, I know. Where did you die?

CORDELIA
Still, still, far wide!

DOCTOR
He's scarce awake. Let him alone awhile.

LEAR
Where have I been? Where am I? Fair daylight?
I am mightily abused. I should e'en die with pity
To see another thus. I know not what to say.
I will not swear these are my hands. Let's see—
I feel this pin prick. Would I were assured
Of my condition.

CORDELIA

                  O look upon me, sir,
And hold your hand in benediction o'er me.
You must not kneel.

LEAR

                    Pray, do not mock me.
I am a very foolish fond old man,
Fourscore and upward, not an hour more nor less;
And, to deal plainly,
I fear I am not in my perfect mind.
Methinks I should know you, and know this man;
Yet I am doubtful, for I am mainly ignorant
What place this is; and all the skill I have
Remembers not these garments; nor I know not
Where I did lodge last night. Do not laugh at me;
For, as I am a man, I think this lady
To be my child Cordelia.

CORDELIA

             And so I am! I am!

LEAR

Be your tears wet? Yes, faith. I pray weep not.
If you have poison for me, I will drink it.
I know you do not love me; for your sisters
Have (as I do remember) done me wrong.
You have some cause, they have not.

CORDELIA

                 No cause, no cause.

Comment

In its title, in the topiary of its rhymes and stanzas, and in the terrible ease, the readiness of its utterance—a man speaking out of his tormented heart, directly, knowingly—Hecht's poem carries a resonance of the Metaphysicals, an echo of what Professor Cruttwell calls the "Shakespearean Moment," that interval in our literary history when there is to be heard—in Donne and Herbert, in Shakespeare increasingly—a certain ironic tension in the utterance, a capacity to extend the voice beyond any one tonality, any uniform design, to a more inclusive register than genre—meditative lyric, grotesque tragedy, miracle play, morality or mystery—had hitherto afforded. For "The Vow" begins with a miscarriage and a quotation from Isaiah, glances at Dante and glares at Santa Claus, mockingly invokes Doctors of Science and meekly invites the ancient Greek wisdom, advice given first by Silenus to Midas and echoed since by Aristotle and Nietzsche: *the best is not to have been born*; the poem closes (like *Lear*, after "the consent of flesh and a midwinter storm") on a quotation from Zechariah entirely relevant, in its context, to the widened range of the matter:

In all the land, saith the Lord, two parts therein shall be cut off and die; but the third shall be left therein.

And I will bring the third part through the fire, and will refine them as silver is refined, and will try them as gold is tried: they shall call on my name, and I will hear them.

A poetry which can gain access to such utterance, such variant and indeed opposing *sagesse*, can aspire to stand beside the supreme Shakespearean moment: a language of monosyllables mostly, discourse which has come through the refining fire to the kind of simplicity no literature except the Bible, translated at this time, ever approached. Like the play, the poem is "about" creative suffering, about the discovery of a capacity for faith born of disillusionment, anguish, and sympathy. Lear's summative line—the center indeed of the entire situation and role and play, for once it is answered the play is done: "Would I were assured / Of my condition"—is the purgatory through which he must pass, stripped of kingship, fatherhood, humanity even, and such assurance is the purgatorial fire which Hecht pursues, to which he vows adherence: a pledge of faith to what may come after "the dead thing" is the pledge Lear too will give, the promise which, with Cordelia's forgiveness ("No cause, no cause"), are the two distinctively human acts, for by them we are differentiated from the nature that generates us. We can promise, and we can forgive—even ourselves.

*Daryl
Hine*

THE WAVE

Suddenly it was quiet as a Sunday,
That extra day when nothing is permitted,
The first or last, whichever you prefer;
Nothing now rolled out her long drawn sway.
The bay was like a vacant nautilus
That held in vain a secret of the sea.
Even dumb things were listening: the trees,
Sentinels of the shore, had ceased their
        signals,
The insects grew self-conscious and fell silent.
    Echo was dead. Dead,

Yet I think we all had the impression
That something would come to us on the
        water,
Music or a message or a god.
Yes, and this held all of our attention,
What was to come, whom, we must wait and
        see.
The afternoon was literally breathless,
Wide awake . . . Soon the promiscuous tide
As if plucked by conscience left the beach,
With a sigh the ocean fled away
    From many a strange bed.

And to be sure it was something shocking
To see the submarine groves' unguessed-at
        grottos
Naked, and the shame of the sea creatures
Exposed amid the wrack of rock and weed.
At the same time, as at a theatre
To warn of the beginning of a play,

There were three knocks, not loud or close
        together,
Distinct and distant, like that and that and
        that,
A reiterated hint to imitate
    The water's get-away:

As if across the empty sea came pirates
Guided by the inner vision of their kind
From the vague extremities that lie
Frozen half the time and furious,
Marked on no map or marked to be forgotten,
Realms of what use to the imagination?
Conventional antipodes of the exotic,
Without a name almost—without fuss or
        motive,
Without a wind through unimpeding calm
    Into the white bay.

I wanted to write it down in my diary
Then and there, this unexceptional moment,
Unique because like every other moment,
It yet had taught me what a moment was.
But even as I wished for pen and paper—
The smooth manila sand, the ink dark sea—
What could I say of an event where nothing
        happened
Save . . . ? I turned to my obstinate
        companions,
Waiting it seemed for wave, shipwreck or
        ransom,
    They stood on the shore mum

Like a person standing before a door,
Listening maybe, that they fear to open,
Which will open of its own accord presently
        inward,
Aware of the vanity of every act.
One watched—the track of the sea, was it
        coming nearer?
Her back to us another, simpler, stared,
The faraway half focused in her eye.
Some swore or prayed—I could see their lips
        moving.
Someone moved his hands in isolate
        absolution
    Or traced a Te Deum.

What happened next do I want to remember?
Perhaps we ran, perhaps we stood our ground
And the ground removed till safe and sound
        we arrived,
Ashamed to count ourselves, for some were
        missing.

Nor could we after witnesses agree
Just how the others met their martyrdom.
The seismographic report said a sea tremor,
The serious minded saw an act of God,
Both inferring further catastrophe
    Certain and sorry.

Whether those horses rode upon the wave
As some pretend, or whether the earth
        yawned,
As well she might in immemorial boredom,
The mess tomorrow saw upon the strand,
The common stock in trade of dogs and gulls,
The picnic drowned, dead bodies, dying fish,
Rubbish and sea things never seen before—
So the memorabilia of the flood,
God's interrupted wish-fulfillment, told
    Some of the story.

Théophile
de Viau

—

ODE

Un corbeau devant moy croasse,
Une ombre offusque mes regards;
Deux bellettes et deux renards
Traversent l'endroit où je passe;
Les pieds faillent à mon cheval,
Mon laquay tombe du haut mal;
J'entends craqueter le tonnerre;
Un esprit se presente à moy;
J'oy Charon qui m'appelle à soy,
Je voy le centre de la terre.

Ce ruisseau remonte en sa source;
Un boeuf gravit sur un clocher;
Le sang coule de ce rocher;
Un aspic s'accouple d'une ourse;
Sur le haut d'une vieille tour
Un serpent deschire un vautour;
Le feu brusle dedans la glace;
Je voy la Lune qui va cheoir;
Cest arbre est sorty de sa place.

Comment /

Burned in effigy, his books condemned, dead at thirty-six, Théophile de Viau is a Byronic figure—exiled for libertinage (a translation of Plato); accused of homosexuality (in 1620 a crime of *lèse-majesté*, an offense against the king's body); persecuted for atheism (the record of his trial deserves to stand beside Jeanne d'Arc's). Or rather, Byron resumes the convention, mediates between Théophile and Rimbaud as the type of the *poète maudit*. Heretical, even blasphemous his opinions may have been; subversive, certainly, his example; yet what rescues Théophile from the shelves of poets we need not read because they have done our living for us, what *salvages* his poetry is its invocation of an oneiric universe, the first French annexation of the dream to the lyric. A disputed dialectics of sleep and waking, of reality and imagination, of wisdom and folly imbues this poetry—a metaphysical vertigo. What we take for reality is perhaps no more than illusion, Théophile concedes, but who knows if what we take for illusion is not also, frequently, reality? The waking ego seems no less fantastic and monstrous than the subject of the dream, and all existence is susceptible of that reversible ambiguity which Théophile expresses here in the theme of hallucination.

Exorcism, therapeutics, the poem *contra naturam* may well bear as its motto Gracian's remark often quoted at the period, "We cannot see clearly the things of this world save by considering them conversely to what they are." Hine makes his own this supremely baroque instance, establishes himself at the hinge moment between dream and waking—between the incantatory bestiary of Bosch, say, and "the common stock in trade of dogs and gulls." And from that vantage, that peculiar passivity of the obsessive observer, he remarks all the mature banalities his wit helps him to, never missing a trick ("Rubbish and sea things never seen before"), as well as the implacable follies to come ("further catastrophe / Certain and sorry"). This world of "The Wave," however miraculous, however mesmeric, is not a world glorified by the divine, but rather an experience of that tremendous suspension of belief, the impending moment when all things are possible, all signs may be reversed, and the self—the recording self:

> *I wanted to write it down in my diary*
> *Then and there, this unexceptional moment,*
> *Unique because like every other moment,*
> *It yet had taught me what a moment was*

the self-as-subject is for that moment elided, stranded or floated above mere identity, so that in its place the language itself speaks ("the memorabilia [. . .] told / Some of the story"), comprehensive, metamorphic, incandescent.

Daniel
Hoffman

THE CITY OF SATISFACTIONS

As I was travelling toward the city of
     satisfactions
On my employment, seeking the treasure of
     pleasure,
Laved in the superdome observation car by
     Muzak
Soothed by the cool conditioned and
     reconditioned air,
Sealed in from the smell of the heat and the
     spines
Of the sere mesquite and the seared windblast
     of the sand,
It was conjunction of a want of juicy fruit
And the train's slowdown and stopping at a
     depot
Not listed on the schedule, unnamed by
     platform sign,
That made me step down on the siding
With some change in hand. The newsstand,
     on inspection,
Proved a shed of greyed boards shading
A litter of stale rags.
Turning back, I blanched at the Silent
     Streak: a wink
Of the sun's reflection caught its rear-view
     window
Far down the desert track. I grabbed the
     crossbar
And the handcar clattered. Up and down
It pumped so fast I hardly could grab hold it,
His regal head held proud despite the
     bending
Knees, back-knees, back-knees, back-knees
     propelling.

His eyes bulged beadier than a desert toad's
     eyes.
His huge hands shrank upon the handlebar,
His mighty shoulders shrivelled and his skin
     grew
Wrinkled while I watched the while we
     reeled
Over the mesquite till the train grew
     larger
And pumping knees, back-knees, we stood
     still and
Down on us the train bore,
The furious tipping of the levers unabated
Wrenching my sweating eyes and aching
     armpits,
He leapt on long webbed feet into the
     drainage
Dryditch and the car swung longside on a
     siding
Slowing down beside the Pullman diner
Where the napkined waiter held a tray of
     glasses.
The gamehen steamed crisp-crust behind the
     glass.
I let go of the tricycle and pulled my askew
     necktie,
Pushed through the diner door, a disused
     streetcar,
A Danish half devoured by flies beneath
     specked glass,
Dirty cups on the counter,
A menu, torn, too coffeestained for choices,
     told
In a map of rings my cryptic eyes unspelled

Of something worth the digging for right
    near by
Here just out beyond the two-door shed.
The tracks were gone now but I found a
    shovel,
Made one, that is, from a rusting oildrum
    cover,
A scrap of baling wire, a broken crutch,
And down I heaved on the giving earth and
    rockshards
And a frog drygasped once from a distant
    gulley
And up I spewed the debris in a range
Of peaks I sank beneath and sweated under
    till
One lunge sounded the clunk of iron on brass
And furious scratch and pawing of the
    dryrock
Uncovered the graven chest and the pile of
    earth downslid
While under a lowering sky, sweatwet, I
    grasped and wrestled
The huge chest, lunged and jerked and
    fought it upward
Till it toppled sideways on the sand. I
    smashed it
Open, and it held a barred box. My nails
    broke
On the bars that wouldn't open. I smashed it
Open and it held a locked box. I ripped my
    knuckles
But couldn't wrest that lock off till I smashed
    it
Open and it held a small box worked
In delicate filigree of silver with
A cunning keyhole. But there was no key.
I pried it, ripped my fingers underneath it

But couldn't get it open till I smashed it
Open and it held a little casket
Sealed tight with twisted wires or vines of
    shining
Thread. I bit and tugged and twisted, cracked
    my teeth
But couldn't loose the knot. I smashed it
Open and the top came off, revealing
A tiny casket made of jade. It had
No top, no seam, no turnkey. Thimblesmall
It winked unmoving near the skinbreak
Where steakjuice pulsed and oozed. I thought
    aroma
Sifted, thinning till the dark horizon
Seemed, and then no longer seemed, a trifle
Sweetened. I knelt before
A piece of desert stone. When I have fitted
That stone into its casket, and replaced
The lid and set that casket in its box,
Fitted the broken top and set that box
    within
The box it came in and bent back the bars
And put it in the chest, the chest back in the
    hole,
The peaks around the pit-edge piled back in
    the pit,
Replaced the baling wire and crutch and
    oildrum cover
And pushed back through the diner, will the
    train
Sealed in from the smell of heat and mesquite
Envelop me in Muzak while it swooshes
Past bleak sidings such as I wait on
Nonstop toward the city of satisfactions
    roaring?
If I could only make this broken top
Fit snug back on this casket

Anonymous

—

THIS IS THE KEY
OF THE KINGDOM

This is the Key of the Kingdom;
In that Kingdom is a city;
In that city is a town;
In that town there is a street;
In that street there winds a lane;
In that lane there is a yard;
In that yard there is a house;
In that house there waits a room;
In that room an empty bed;
And on that bed a basket—
A Basket of Sweet Flowers:
  Of Flowers, of Flowers;
  A basket of Sweet Flowers.

Flowers in a basket;
Basket on the bed;
Bed in the chamber;
Chamber in the house;
House in the weedy yard;
Yard in the winding lane;
Lane in the broad street;
Street in the high town;
Town in the city;
City in the Kingdom—
This is the Key of the Kingdom.
  Of the Kingdom this is the Key.

Comment

The point is to get in to where the point is, and then to get out again, to reach a circumference on which any point presents the opportunity of ingress, of egress. To cast off the integument, and then to reassume it, transfigured. In his five books of poems, Hoffman has been concerned, has been obsessed with this matter of entering and leaving, with that discovery of the One Life which lies under the lid of the heterogeneous, and again with the escape from the bound litany into the freedom of "an exhalation of eternity / Desiring nothing."

Like the little counting-verse which holds that offhand secret of all spells, charms, incantations —the unwinding of a spool which thereby gathers its energies, its conjurations, on the other side, the twist which, as the word reminds us, works *twice over*—Hoffman's grand fantasia on themes of urban dispossession suffers (and benefits) from the overdetermination of dreams, the futility of logic. Dantesque, the journey converges upon its center, the decor twitched teasingly away, the personnel elusive, untrustworthy, until we reach the nodal point, "the piece of desert stone" which must then be restored to the very context in which the journey was undertaken (though of course there can be no restoration: too much has been destroyed in order to get there). As he asks his Sisyphean question at the end of his poem, the speaker returns to his mindless, unpersuadable task: the terrible burden of brutality and fierce participation in an old unreasoning order of nature, an old service of life in its ritual sense, wherein the dignity and preservation of the self count for nothing at all. As Hoffman has said, "the ecstasy of religious possession is perilously attained . . . independently of history, of society, of everything in life save itself." Like the traditional verse, Hoffman's oneiric ordeal, a nightmare worthy of one of Poe's victims, must turn chaos into cosmos, and *kairos* into *chronos*, by the mere and mortal process of undoing, then doing up again, thereby analogizing the work of all poetry, all *physis*, which is a movement inward, and a movement outward, an implication and an explication, folding and unfolding. Dismembering is thus revealed to be the matrix of form, for it is in the action of *doing over again* that the significance of what is done and undone may be shown, known, remembered.

John
Hollander

THE NIGHT MIRROR

What it showed was always the same—
A vertical panel with him in it,
Being a horrible bit of movement
At the edge of knowledge, overhanging
The canyons of nightmare. And when the last
Glimpse was enough—his grandmother,
Say, with a blood-red face, rising
From her Windsor chair in the warm lamplight
To tell him something—he would scramble up,
Waiting to hear himself shrieking, and gain
The ledge of the world, his bed, lit by
The pale rectangle of window, eclipsed
By a dark shape, but a shape that moved
And saw and knew and mistook its reflection
In the tall panel on the closet door
For itself. The silver corona of moonlight
That glorified his glimpsed head was enough
To send him back into silences (choosing
Fear in those chasms below), to reject
Freedom of wakeful seeing, believing
And feeling, for peace and the bondage to horrors
Welling up only from deep within
That dark planet head, spinning beyond
The rim of the night mirror's range, huge
And cold, on the pillow's dark side.

Percy Shelley

—

THE TWO SPIRITS: AN ALLEGORY

FIRST SPIRIT

O thou, who plumed with strong desire
    Wouldst float above the earth, beware!
A shadow tracts thy flight of fire—
        Night is coming!
    Bright are the regions of the air,
And among the winds and beams
    It were delight to wander there—
        Night is coming!

SECOND SPIRIT

The deathless stars are bright above;
    If I would cross the shade of night,
Within my heart is the lamp of love,
        And that is day!
    And the moon will smile with gentle light
On my golden plumes where'er they move;
    The meteors will linger round my flight,
        And make night day.

FIRST SPIRIT

But if the whirlwinds of darkness waken
    Hail, and lightning, and stormy rain;
See, the bounds of the air are shaken—
        Night is coming!
    The red swift clouds of the hurricane
Yon declining sun have overtaken,
    The clash of the hail sweeps over the plain—
        Night is coming!

SECOND SPIRIT

I see the light, and I hear the sound;
   I'll sail on the flood of the tempest dark,
With the calm within and the light around
     Which makes night day:
And thou, when the gloom is deep and stark,
Look from thy dull earth, slumber-bound,
   My moon-like flight thou then mayst mark
     On high, far away.

——————

Some say there is a precipice
   Where one vast pine is frozen to ruin
O'er piles of snow and chasms of ice
     Mid Alpine mountains;
   And that the languid storm pursuing
That wingèd shape, for ever flies
   Round those hoar branches, aye renewing
     Its aery fountains.

Some say when nights are dry and clear,
   And the death-dews sleep on the morass,
Sweet whispers are heard by the traveller,
     Which make night day:
And a silver shape like his early love doth pass
Upborne by her wild and glittering hair
   And when he awakes on the fragrant grass
     He finds night day.

Comment |

More surely, more civilly than even Byron, Shelley articulates that Faustian impulse which has become, with us, almost fustian: to divide against ourselves. We are forever sundering into Infernal Parts an identity else dismissed as unconscious and therefore unworthy (Hollander's subject chooses "to reject / Freedom of wakeful seeing, believing / And feeling"). In the beautiful late lyric—though for Shelley "late" means merely "too late," means "posthumous"—the imminence of darkness so exultantly prophesied by the first spirit is by the second welcomed as the cause of transformation, the ground of possible mastery. The possibility, in both poets, is all interior: "Within my heart is the lamp of love, / And that is day!" Shelley's second spirit insists, as Hollander's wise child insists, on the "bondage to horrors welling up from deep within," and when the choice is made, the dialogue completed, some myth of reconcilement is offered, or of metamorphosis. "The traveller"—who is the reader, the poet, the agent *within* whom the spirits speak against each other—"wakes on the fragrant grass" and "finds night day." This is what Keats intends, surely, in his letter of five years before Shelley's poem when he says "the Imagination may be compared to Adam's dream—he awoke and found it truth."

More drastic, but with the same sense of necessary loss, Hollander celebrates a world of which we are, by living in it, dispossessed; a world of negatives, of failures and obscurations summoning up the doom which in the poem subsides, allayed by its own domination. The little boy in "The Night Mirror" will waken to day only upon the acknowledgment of "horrors," the world darkened by his own shadow. He goes to sleep choosing the mind's monsters over those of reality, even of mirrored reality (not to mention the lunar grandmother "with a blood-red face, rising," like Shelley's "red swift clouds of the hurricane," to tell the poet "something"), inaugurating a delicate dialectic of light, reflection, darkness, and dream. Inexorable in its syntax, Hollander's final ten-line sentence proceeds from "silver corona" to its "dark side," riverine, melodramatic, high, to a visionary climax worthy of Shelley's "silver shape." The modern poet's sentence is hard because it is a death sentence, and Hollander will not let his lines go until they have turned and, grammatically, blessed him. Shelley's two spirits may say, with him, that this is the transfiguration "whose end I trudge toward, my shadow and I annihilating each other as we approach," in order that all the resources of making may fulfill the negative by reflections of return, by the mirror of verse, of revision, recuperation, getting back—not only finding but *making* night day.

Richard
Howard

GIOVANNI DA FIESOLE ON THE SUBLIME *or*
FRA ANGELICO'S "LAST JUDGMENT"

How to behold what cannot be held?
Start from the center and from all that
lies or flies or merely rises left
of center. You may have noticed how
Hell, in these affairs, is on the right
invariably (though for an inside Judge,
of course, that would be the left. And we
are not inside). I have no doctrine
intricate enough for Hell, which I leave
in its own right, where it will be left.

Right down the center, then, in two rows,
run nineteen black holes, their square lids off;
also one sarcophagus, up front.
Out of these has come the world; out of
that coffin, I guess, the Judge above
the world. Nor is my doctrine liable
to smooth itself out for the blue ease
of Heaven outlining one low hill
against the sky at the graveyard's end
like a woman's body—a hill like Eve.

Some of us stand, still, at the margin
of this cemetery, marvelling
that no more than a mortared pavement can
separate us from the Other Side
which numbers as many nuns and priests

(even Popes and Empresses!) as ours.
The rest, though, stirring to a music
that our startled blood remembers now,
embrace each other or the Angels
of this green place: the dancing begins.

We dance in a circle of bushes,
red and yellow roses, round a pool
of green water. There is one lily,
gold as a lantern in the dark grass,
and all the trees accompany us
with gestures of fruition. We stop!
The ring of bodies opens where a last
Angel, in scarlet, hands us on. Now
we go, we are leaving this garden
of colors and gowns. We walk into

A light falling upon us, falling
out of the great rose gate upon us,
light so thick we cannot trust our eyes
to walk into it so. We lift up
our hands then and walk into the light.
How to behold what cannot be held?
Make believe you hold it, no longer
lighting but light, and walk into that
gold success. The world must be its own
witness, we judge ourselves, raise your hands.

Robert Browning

from
FRA LIPPO LIPPI

                              . . . I shall paint
God in the midst, Madonna and her babe,
Ringed by a bowery flowery angel-brood,
Lilies and vestments and white-faces, sweet
As puff on puff of grated orris-root
When ladies crowd to church at midsummer.
And then i' the front, of course, a saint or two—
Saint John, because he saves the Florentines,
Saint Ambrose, who puts down in black and white
The convent's friends and gives them a long day,
And Job, I must have him there past mistake,
The man of Uz (and Us without the z,
Painters who need his patience). Well, all these
Secured at their devotion, up shall come
Out of a corner when you least expect
As one by a dark stair into a great light,
Music and talking, who but Lippo! I!—
Mazed, motionless and moonstruck—I'm the man!
Back I shrink—what is this I see and hear?
I, caught up with my monk's-things by mistake,
My old serge gown and rope that goes all round,
I, in this presence, this pure company!
Where's a hole, where's a corner for escape?
Then steps a sweet angelic slip of a thing
Forward, puts out a soft palm—'Not so fast!'
—Addresses the celestial presence, 'nay—
'He made you and devised you, after all,
'Though he's none of you! Could Saint John there draw—
'His camel-hair make up a painting-brush?
'We come to brother Lippo for all that,
'*Iste perfecit opus!*'

Comment |

There is a painting, a *Last Judgment*, say, or a *Coronation of the Virgin*, to be seen in the world—in Florence, which is the world for the two painters, Fra Angelico, Fra Lippo Lippi—and two poets, compelled into acknowledgment, seek to make terms with the painting; their poems are the terms they come to, of course. By recognition of taste and talent, by temperament in fact, Browning sets to work behind the painting—he writes his poem *toward* the creating of the picture, whereas Howard begins in front of the painting—he writes his poem *from* the created picture. The phenomenon suggests, in the Victorian, a certain pre-emptive force, an eagerness to perform, while in the contemporary there is a corresponding passivity, an assumption that the picture, as it stands now, already, will disclose its significance.

In both poets, whatever the discrepancy in imaginative strength, in conceptual strategy, there is one remarkable similarity in executive attitude—it is their evidently shared trust in what Yeats called natural momentum in the syntax, a cumulus he said made it possible for a poem to carry "any amount of elaborate English." And elaborate the English is, faceted with turns and returns ("Hell, which I leave / in its own right, where it will be left"), with an alliteration struggling to become the master-principle of the meter ("Mazed, motionless and moonstruck— I'm the man!"), and with a playful consciousness of the diversions to be made available in the difference between the language written and the language spoken ("The man of Uz (and Us without the z, / Painters who need his patience),*" or again: *"How to behold what cannot be held? / Make believe you hold it"*). The confidence shared, the saving grace, is all in the capacity of language itself—compulsively qualified, idiosyncratic in address—to carry the impulse, the effort of the poem by the *energeia* words hold within themselves, by the dynamics they generate "among one another" line by line, a secret plot.

When Ruskin complained, as everyone did, about his obscurity, Browning replied for once with an insight framing the perspective by which both himself and Howard, poets of apostrophe rather than of silence, of utterance rather than of inference, may well, may *best* be regarded: "You ought, I think, to keep pace with the thought tripping from ledge to ledge of my 'glaciers', as you call them, not stand poking your alpenstock into the holes, and demonstrating that no fool could have stood there—suppose he sprang there? . . . The whole is all but a simultaneous feeling with me."

Richard
Hugo

THE CHURCH ON COMIAKEN HILL

The lines are keen against today's bad sky
about to rain. We're white and understand
why Indians sold butter for the funds
to build this church. Four hens and a rooster
huddle on the porch. We are dark
and know why no one climbed to pray. The priest
who did his best to imitate a bell
watched the river, full of spirits, coil
below the hill, relentless for the bay.

123

A church abandoned to the wind is portent.
In high wind, ruins make harsh music.
The priest is tending bar. His dreams have paid
outrageous fees for stone and mortar.
His eyes are empty as a chapel
roofless in a storm. Greek temples seem
the same as forty centuries ago.
If we used one corner for a urinal,
he wouldn't swear we hadn't worshipped here.

The chickens cringe. Rain sprays chaos where
the altar and the stained glass would have gone
had Indians not eaten tribal cows
one hungry fall. Despite the chant,
salmon hadn't come. The first mass
and a phone line cursed the river.
If rain had rhythm, it would not be Latin.

Children do not wave as we drive out.
Like these graves ours may go unmarked.
Can we best be satisfied when dead
with daffodils for stones? These Indians—
whatever they once loved or used for God—
the hill—the river—the bay burned by the moon—
they knew that when you die you lose your name.

William Wordsworth

—

from
LINES COMPOSED
A FEW MILES
ABOVE TINTERN
ABBEY

. . . For thou art with me here upon the banks
Of this fair river; thou my dearest Friend,
My dear, dear Friend; and in thy voice I catch
The language of my former heart, and read
My former pleasures in the shooting lights
Of thy wild eyes. Oh! yet a little while
May I behold in thee what I was once,
My dear, dear Sister! and in this prayer I make,
Knowing that Nature never did betray
The heart that loved her; 'tis her privilege,
Through all the years of this our life, to lead
From joy to joy: for she can so inform
The mind that is within us, so impress
With quietness and beauty, and so feed
With lofty thoughts, that neither evil tongues,
Rash judgments, nor the sneers of selfish men,
Nor greetings where no kindness is, nor all
The dreary intercourse of daily life,
Shall e'er prevail against us, or disturb
Our cheerful faith, that all which we behold
Is full of blessings. Therefore let the moon
Shine on thee in thy solitary walk;
And let the misty mountain-winds be free
To blow against thee: and, in after years,
When these wild ecstasies shall be matured
Into a sober pleasure; when thy mind
Shall be a mansion for all lovely forms,
Thy memory be as a dwelling-place
For all sweet sounds and harmonies; oh! then,
If solitude, or fear, or pain, or grief,
Should be thy portion, with what healing thoughts
Of tender joy wilt thou remember me,
And these my exhortations! Nor, perchance—
If I should be where I no more can hear
Thy voice, nor catch from thy wild eyes these gleams
Of past existence—wilt thou then forget
That on the banks of this delightful stream
We stood together . . .

Comment /

Ironies are not so easy as they at first appear. When De Quincey grimaced at the senile, wasted parody of Dorothy Wordsworth, wheeled out of her Grasmere Cottage blind and mewling, he sneered, "Nature never did betray the heart that loved her," and in mocking Wordsworth he was making the same error we are liable to in misreading Hugo's "river, full of spirits, / coil below the hill, relentless for the bay" as a condemnation, a revulsion even. Everything depends, in Wordsworth as in Hugo, on how we take *betrayal*—the point is that no covenant is made with nature, no program for comfort, for recourse; merely for truth, for keeping faith with the past, that terrible memory, acknowledged.

In Hugo's spirit, which like Wordsworth's is always a spirit of place, landscape or location itself enacts what it cannot enable: "on cliffs above the town, high homes disdain: what is not Victorian below / but Indian or cruel." Obsessively committed, like Wordsworth—however various the object of his commitment—Hugo's concern is the unenviable, the unvisited, even the uninviting, which he may or must invest with his own deprivations, his own private war.

The distinctness of impulse in the language, the recognizably Wordsworthian movement organized in unitary syllables by the craving mind:

> *These Indians—*
> *whatever they once loved or used for God—*
> *the hill—the river—the bay burned by the moon—*
> *they knew that when you die you lose your name.*

this credible richness is related to, even derived from, the poverty of the place, local emanation free (or freed) to be the poet's own. Thus the loving heart is never betrayed. What startles, then reassures in all this canon of the inconsolable, the unsanctified, the dispossessed, is Hugo's analogy of language to experience, his poetics. If significance is to be discovered in a world of refusals, then the method as well as the madness must be policed by the negative: demands of resistance overcome, rhythm completed, meaning presumed which we call *form*. Neither silence nor screaming would generate this utterance, but alone that submission to negation, sacrifice, denial, and constraint which makes up the entire justice (and generosity) of prosody. It is no accident, it is a kind of fate, that we must develop a *negative* in order to produce a true *image*.

Donald
Justice

MEN AT FORTY

Men at forty
Learn to close softly
The doors to rooms they will not be
Coming back to.

At rest on a stair landing,
They feel it moving
Beneath them now like the deck of a ship,
Though the swell is gentle.

And deep in mirrors
They rediscover
The face of the boy as he practices tying
His father's tie there in secret

And the face of that father,
Still warm with the mystery of lather.
They are more fathers than sons themselves now.
Something is filling them, something

That is like the twilight sound
Of the crickets, immense,
Filling the woods at the foot of the slope
Behind their mortgaged houses.

William
Shakespeare

SONNET CIV

To me, fair friend, you never can be old,
For as you were when first your eye I ey'd,
Such seems your beauty still. Three winters cold
Have from the forests shook three summers' pride,
Three beauteous springs to yellow autumns turn'd
In process of the seasons have I seen,
Three April perfumes in three hot Junes burn'd,
Since first I saw you fresh, which yet are green.
Ah, yet doth beauty, like a dial hand,
Steal from his figure, and no pace perceiv'd!
So your sweet hue, which methinks still doth stand,
Hath motion, and mine eye may be deceiv'd;
    For fear of which, hear this, thou age unbred:
    Ere you were born was beauty's summer dead.

Comment | In the center of Donald Justice's poem is a mirror, the middle of the body's journey back into boyhood, forward into a paternity now its own. By means of this reflection, the consciousness held captive in the impounding, aging self is made to know that because it *is* conscious it is a captive, *captivated* in precisely the sense (or the two senses) that Narcissus is subject to himself. The word in the poem that bears the entire weight of what is said to be gradually "filling" the man at forty is of course *mortgaged*—pledged to death, and it operates within the easy diction of the poem as a difficult reminder at the close, just as in Shakespeare's sonnet the signal is sounded at the start, the *poetic* signal of something to watch out for: "when first your *eye I ey'd*."

Indeed, it is Justice's poem with its telescoping of father and man and boy into the same mirrored enigma which affords us a discovery of what all the sonnets addressed to the "fair friend" signify: they are in fact the poems of Narcissus to himself (hence the triple "I" at the outset), the ego discovering in itself that "process of the seasons" which the poet is yet willing to submit to as a part of great creating nature, confident of the rightness of natural order rather than of its outrage. This is one of the rare sonnets in the series whose final couplet is not supererogatory but crucial to the poem's sense, for it suggests, it enforces even, the repetition-compulsion which is the ground bass of this group, the fact that life renews itself in a cycle larger than that of individual personal lives. There is a splendid symmetry which has surely not escaped Justice, in the role of the word "dead" at the end of Shakespeare's poem and of the word "mortgaged" at the end of his own—though of course we must note a larger trust, a grander resonance in Shakespeare's "dead" which includes rather than merely isolates experience—this is the death which contains the seeds of life, not an expiration merely. We are told that beauty's summer was dead before the self even began to age—and we are thereby empowered to infer that there will be another spring, that the dial hand *must* turn. Donald Justice will allow no more than a "twilight sound," a "mortgaged house"—his Narcissus is deciduous, compacted, darkened, doomed.

Galway
Kinnell

THE PATH AMONG THE STONES

1

On the path winding
upward, toward the high valley
of waterfalls and flooded, hoof-shattered
meadows of spring,
where fish-roots boil
in the last grails of light on the water,
and vipers pimpled with urges to fly
drape the black stones hissing *pheet! pheet!*—land
of quills
and inkwells of skulls filled with black water—

I come to a field
glittering with the thousand sloughed skins
of arrowheads, stones
which shuddered and leapt forth
to give themselves into the broken hearts
of the living,
who gave themselves back, broken, to the stone.

2

I close my eyes:
on the heat-rippled beaches
where the hills came down to the sea,
the luminous
beach dust pounded out of funeral shells,
I can see
them living without me, dying
without me, the wing
and egg

shaped stones, broken
war-shells of slain fighting conches,
dog-eared immortality shells
in which huge constellations of slime, by the full moon,
writhed one more
coat of invisibility on a speck of sand,

and the agates knocked
from circles scratched into the dust
with the click
of a wishbone breaking, inward-swirling
globes biopsied out of sunsets never to open again,

and that wafer-stone
which skipped ten times across
the water, suddenly starting to run as it went under,
and the zeroes it left,
that met
and passed into each other, they themselves
smoothing themselves from the water. . . .

3

I walk out from myself,
among the stones of the field,
each sending up its ghost-bloom
into the starlight, to float out
over the trees, seeking to be one
with the unearthly fires kindling and dying

in space—and falling back, knowing
the sadness of the wish
to alight
back among the glitter of bruised ground,
the stones holding between pasture and field,
the great, granite nuclei,
glimmering, even they, with ancient inklings of madness and war.

4

A way opens
at my feet. I go down
the night-lighted mule-steps into the earth,
the footprints behind me
filling already with pre-sacrificial trills
of canaries, go down
into the unbreathable goaf
of everything I ever craved and lost.

An old man, a stone
lamp at his forehead, squats
by his hell-flames, stirs into
his pot
chopped head
of crow, strings of white light,
opened tail of peacock, dressed
body of canary, robin breast
dragged through the mud of battlefields, wrung-out
blossom of caput mortuum flower—salts
it all down with sand
stolen from the upper bells of hourglasses . . .

Nothing.
Always nothing. Ordinary blood
boiling away in the glare of the brow lamp.

5

And yet, no,
perhaps not nothing. Perhaps
not ever nothing. In clothes
woven out of the blue spittle
of snakes, I crawl up: I find myself alive
in the whorled
archway of the fingerprint of all things,
skeleton groaning,
blood-strings wailing the wail of all things.

6

The witness trees heal
their scars at the flesh fire,
the flame
rises off the bones,
the hunger
to be new lifts off
my soul, an eerie blue light blooms
on all the ridges of the world. Somewhere
in the legends of blood sacrifice
the fatted calf
takes the bonfire into his arms, and *he*
burns *it*.

7

As above: the last scattered stars
kneel down in the star-form of the Aquarian age:
a splash
on the top of the head,
on the grass of this earth even the stars love, splashes of the sacred waters . . .

So below: in the graveyard
the lamps start lighting up, one for each of us,
in all the windows
of stone.

Walt Whitman

from
SONG OF MYSELF

5

I believe in you my soul, the other I am must not abase itself to you,
And you must not be abased to the other.
Loafe with me on the grass, loose the stop from your throat,
Not words, not music or rhyme I want, not custom or lecture, not even the best,
Only the lull I like, the hum of your valvèd voice.

I mind how once we lay such a transparent summer morning
How you settled your head athwart my hips and gently turn'd over upon me,
And parted the shirt from my bosom-bone, and plunged your tongue to my bare-stript heart,
And reach'd till you felt my beard, and reach'd till you held my feet.

Swiftly arose and spread around me the peace and knowledge that pass all the argument of the
        earth,

And I know that the hand of God is the promise of my own,
And I know that the spirit of God is the brother of my own,
And that all the men ever born are also my brothers, and the women my sisters and lovers,
And that a kelson of the creation is love,
And limitless are leaves stiff or drooping in the fields,
And brown ants in the little wells beneath them,
And mossy scabs of the worm fence, heap'd stones, elder, mullein and poke-weed.

24

. . . I believe in the flesh and the appetites,
Seeing, hearing, feeling, are miracles, and each part and tag of me is a miracle.

139

Divine am I inside and out, and I make holy whatever I touch or am touch'd from,
The scent of these arm-pits aroma finer than prayer,
This head more than churches, bibles, and all the creeds.

If I worship one thing more than another it shall be the spread of my own body, or any part of it,
Translucent mould of me it shall be you!
Shaded ledges and rests it shall be you!
Firm masculine colter it shall be you!
Whatever goes to the tilth of me it shall be you!
You my rich blood! your milky stream pale strippings of my life!
Breast that presses against other breasts it shall be you!
My brain it shall be your occult convolutions!
Root of wash'd sweet-flag! timorous pond-snipe! nest of guarded duplicate eggs! it shall be you!
Mix'd tussled hay of head, beard, brawn, it shall be you!
Trickling sap of maple, fibre of manly wheat, it shall be you!
Sun so generous it shall be you!
Vapors lighting and shading my face it shall be you!
You sweaty brooks and dews it shall be you!
Winds whose soft-tickling genitals rub against me it shall be you!
Broad muscular fields, branches of live oak, loving lounger in my winding paths, it shall be you!
Hands I have taken, face I have kiss'd, mortal I have ever touch'd, it shall be you.

46
. . . My signs are a rain-proof coat, good shoes, and a staff cut from the woods,
No friend of mine takes his ease in my chair,
I have no chair, no church, no philosophy,
I lead no man to a dinner-table, library, exchange,

But each man and each woman of you I lead upon a knoll,
My left hand hooking you round the waist,
My right hand pointing to landscapes of continents and the public road.

Not I, not any one else can travel that road for you,
You must travel it for yourself.

It is not far, it is within reach,
Perhaps you have been on it since you were born and did not know,
Perhaps it is everywhere on water and on land.

Shoulder your duds dear son, and I will mine, and let us hasten forth,
Wonderful cities and free nations we shall fetch as we go.

If you tire, give me both burdens, and rest the chuff of your hand on my hip,
And in due time you shall repay the same service to me,
For after we start we never lie by again.

This day before dawn I ascended a hill and look'd at the crowded heaven,
And I said to my spirit *When we become the enfolders of those orbs, and the pleasure
        and knowledge of everything in them, shall we be fill'd and satisfied then?*
And my spirits said *No, we but level that lift to pass and continue beyond.*

You are also asking me questions and I hear you,
I answer that I cannot answer, you must find out for yourself.

Sit a while dear son,
Here are the biscuits to eat and here is milk to drink,
But as soon as you sleep and renew yourself in sweet clothes, I kiss you with a good-by kiss and
        open the gate for your egress hence.

Long enough have you dream'd contemptible dreams,
Now I wash the gum from your eyes,
You must habit yourself to the dazzle of the light and of every moment of your life.

Comment /

The same encircling, embracing lust for integrity, for entirety (which does not mean everything there is—it means the *wholeness* of whatever there may be) which leads Kinnell to choose "The Song of Myself" entire as his preference, and only concessively to choose the superb portions of it given here, torn up by the roots—commands his own poetry and his choice of it as well: "The Path among the Stones" is the ninth and penultimate section of *The Book of Nightmares*, and indeed both poets tend—are tempted—to enlist whatever they can seize in order to bring themselves home to . . . themselves. They are poets of the One Book, a fervent Scripture which might apprehend what is the poet's body, the changing earth, and the human mind. But not human memory: memory and all it implies of convention, decorum, recurrence, and discretion are discredited—as Whitman said, "I and mine do not convince by arguments, similes, rhymes, / We convince by our presence." Both men write poetry, they do not write poems; body-English, not verses. And their poetry is a seizure indeed, each canto of it a fit, as the name used to be, a spasm, an ecstatic exploration in the first sense of the word: a calling-out upon the world's otherness. "The death of the self I seek," Kinnell has written, "in poetry and out of poetry, is not a drying up or withering. It is a death, yes, but a death out of which one might hope to be reborn more giving, more alive, more open, more related to the natural life."

How close, how nearly coincident this program brings him to Whitman, for whom the trembling emblem is no poet but Orpheus! Harsher, more willing to sacrifice himself to his enterprise than the shrewder, dubious Whitman ("I know perfectly well my own egotism, / Know my omnivorous lines and must not write any less"), Kinnell is as duly empowered to render justice to the physical world, "the irretrievable": the same stark stones, the same speckled eggs, the same sexual flesh are not so much sentenced or even saluted here as they are given way to. More drastically than Whitman (Kinnell's *natures mortes* have all died a violent death), the lines are forever opening up, so that what is left behind, untended, assumes a charred aspect. Kinnell's whole man engorges the world, other men, even the whole woman, but the process is one of nightmare, not greeting; his poetry is an interval between burning and burning.

Carolyn
Kizer

THE COPULATING GODS

Brushing back the curls from your famous brow,
Lingering over the prominent temple vein
Purple as Aegean columns in the dawn,
Calm now, I ponder how self-consciously
The gods must fornicate.
It is that sense of unseen witness:
Those mortals with whom we couple or have coupled,
Clinging to our swan-suits, our bull-skins,
Our masquerades in coin and shrubbery.

We were their religion before they were born.
The spectacle of our carnality
Confused them into spiritual lust.
The headboard of our bed became their altar,
Rare nectar, shared, a common sacrament.
The wet drapery of our sheets, moulded
To noble thighs, is made the basis
For a whole new aesthetic:
God is revealed as the first genius.

Men continue to invent our histories,
Deny our equal pleasure in each other.
Club-foot, nymphomaniac, they dub us,
Then fabricate the net that God will cast
Over our raptures: we, trussed up like goats,
Paraded past the searchlights of the sky
By God himself, the ringmaster and cuckold,
Amidst a thunderous laughter and applause.

Tracing again the bones of your famous face,
I know we are not their history but our myth.
Heaven prevents time; and our astral raptures
Float buoyant in the universe. Come, kiss!
Come, swoon again, we who invented dying
And the whole alchemy of resurrection.
They will concoct a scripture explaining this.

Mark
Alexander
Boyd

—

VENUS
AND CUPID

Frae bank to bank, frae wood to wood I rin
Owrhailit with my feeble fantasie,
Like til a leaf that fallis from a tree,
Or til a reed owrblawin with the win.
Two gads guides me: the ane of them is blin,
Yea, and a bairn brocht up in vanitie;
The nixt a wife ingenerit of the sea
and lichter nor a dauphin with her fin.

Unhappie is the man for evermair
That tills the sand and sawis in the air;
But twice unhappier is he, I lairn,
that feedis in his hairt a mad desire,
And follows on a woman throu the fire,
Led by a blin, and teachit by a bairn.

---

owrhailit overwhelmed (line 2)
ingenerit engendered (line 7)
lichter nor lighter than (line 8)

Comment

Born a year before Shakespeare and dying in his canonical mid-thirties (Byron, Schubert, Jesus), Boyd was regarded as one of the finest Latin poets of his day (a day which included George Buchanan!) and was evidently an admirer of the Ronsard who had written:

> Que l'homme se deçoit
> Quand plein d'erreur un aveugle il reçoit
> Pour sa conduite, un enfant pour son maistre

echoed here in the final lines of the finest sonnet in the Scots language, a poem which welcomes the conventions of prosody and passion, which *requires* such conventions in order to deliver the full force of feeling. Only forms can engage the formless; only myth can engross and accommodate chaos.

Focusing her interest on Figure rather than on Character ("the prominent temple vein / Purple as Aegean columns in the dawn"—that is Adonis transformed into an acropolis!), aspiring to something larger and more luminous than life, though composed, surely, of just the details (swan-suits and shrubbery, "the wet drapery of our sheets") we are accustomed to reckon with in accounts of selfhood smaller than life, Carolyn Kizer's copulating gods are not merely Hephaistos and Aphrodite, as we might first think from their nicknames, "club-foot, nymphomaniac"; they are rather human beings who can speak so ("we, trussed up like goats, / Paraded past the searchlights of the sky") only when they are caught in some energy of apprehension, some fit of facture which transcends the fatal et cetera of things. It is the lover, the artist, the poet who is—now and then—the god; Byron the clubfoot, not Hephaistos, and at such times, this poet says, "I know we are not their history but our myth." As in all Carolyn Kizer's poems, but most intricately specific here in its chastised relation to the godhead proposed by the Scots goliard, the voice of the copulating gods is the voice of a despairing illumination, wedding chaos and failure, conjugating pain and farce in the recognition of shared contours, of welcomed limits. So much for my "scripture explaining," as every Jesus has his Paul, every Byron his Trelawny, the theophany afforded here to Everyman, provided he can acknowledge the unique occasion when he is more than himself, participates in that divine condition which the personal merely hides.

Stanley
Kunitz

ROBIN REDBREAST

It was the dingiest bird
you ever saw, all the color
washed from him, as if
he had been standing in the rain,
friendless and stiff and cold,
since Eden went wrong.
In the house marked For Sale,
where nobody made a sound,
in the room where I lived
with an empty page, I had heard
the squawking of the jays
under the wild persimmons
tormenting him.
So I scooped him up
after they knocked him down,
in league with that ounce of heart
pounding in my palm,
that dumb beak gaping.
Poor thing! Poor foolish life!
without sense enough to stop
running in desperate circles,
needing my lucky help
to toss him back into his element.
But when I held him high,
fear clutched my hand,
for through the hole in his head,
cut whistle-clean . . .
through the old dried wound
between his eyes
where the hunter's brand
had tunneled out his wits . . .
I caught the cold flash of the blue
unappeasable sky.

George
Herbert

—

LOVE

Love bade me welcome: yet my soul drew back,
      Guiltie of dust and sinne.
But quick-ey'd Love, observing me grow slack
      From my first entrance in,
Drew nearer to me, sweetly questioning,
      If I lack'd any thing.

A guest, I answer'd, worthy to be here:
      Love said, You shall be he.
I the unkinde, ungratefull? Ah my deare,
      I cannot look on thee.
Love took my hand, and smiling did reply,
      Who made the eyes but I?

Truth Lord, but I have marr'd them: let my shame
      Go where it doth deserve.
And know you not, sayes Love, who bore the blame?
      My deare, then I will serve.
You must sit down, sayes Love, and taste my meat:
      So I did sit and eat.

Comment |

"His thought has that heat as actually to fuse the words, so that language is wholly flexible in his hands, and his rhyme never stops the progress of the sense," Emerson wrote of Herbert in his *Journal* for 1831 (he was twenty-eight); it was more difficult, perhaps, seeing so keenly, for Emerson to see beyond flexibility to the formal responsibility, to the fact that the rhyme *enabled* the progress, enforced it, made it a progress indeed rather than an exemplification, merely, of Luke 12:37: "Verily I say unto you, that he shall gird himself, and make them to sit down to meat, and will come forth and serve them."

Herbert's poem is a description of the soul's reception into heaven, Kunitz's of the soul's exclusion from it; what signifies (heaven does not much signify, either in the welcoming thither or the ostracism thence) is the matter of tone, in all poetry perhaps the most difficult matter to . . . materialize, to come to terms with, for it seems to defy terms. Yet it is *tone* which makes us able and willing and eager to read the metaphysical, however transcendentally, with the same *fusion* of interests with which we read the modern— it is tone which is the overlap and coincidence of the poet speaking *onto* the page and the poet heard *from* the page. Assuredly the more measures, the more means there are to capture and control and connect the setting down with the picking up, the more possibilities there will be for *tonality*.

What Kunitz does which is so remarkable—it is why he has chosen a lyric explicitly formal to set beside his own, which is formal implicitly— is to invent or invoke an altogether unhearkened set of forms, of conveniences and ardors, by which to govern and even generate his tone, relying chiefly on axiological enjambment, on concealed or at least deferred rhyme (the final sentence which begins with the six-syllable line "But when I held him high" rhymes it nine lines later with the six-syllable line "unappeasable sky"), and most crucially on the complicated sentence—a life sentence, for it is the captivation of the living voice—on baroque syntax looped like an anaconda upon its punctuation and pronouns in such a way that we can find no release from it, once we are within its toils, but at the poem's close. As in the Herbert poem, what matters and murmurs and meanders here is not symbolism, nor even situation ("since Eden went wrong," "without sense enough to stop"—these separate lines are dictatorial in their significations, if we seek to be commanded), but the speaking voice, the temper of the man addressing himself to his heart ("the heart breaks and breaks and lives by breaking," Kunitz has aphorized), the *tone* which is caught by the verse, caught or caught up, recovered from mere utterance, recuperated from the waste of our speech and discovered on the page, line by line—the self disclosing itself by closure, or, as Herbert's Love says in what we used to call a rhetorical question: "Who made the eyes but I?"

Denise Levertov

ADVENT 1966

Because in Vietnam the vision of a Burning Babe
is multiplied, multiplied,
                   the flesh on fire
not Christ's, as Southwell saw it, prefiguring
the Passion upon the Eve of Christmas,

but wholly human and repeated, repeated,
infant after infant, their names forgotten,
their sex unkown in the ashes,
set alight, flaming but not vanishing,
not vanishing as his vision but lingering,

cinders upon the earth or living on
moaning and stinking in hospitals three abed;

because of this my strong sight,
my clear caressive sight, my poet's sight I was given
that it might stir me to song,
is blurred.
               There is a cataract filming over
my inner eyes. Or else a monstrous insect
has entered my head, and looks out
from my sockets with multiple vision,

seeing not the unique Holy Infant
burning sublimely, an imagination of redemption,
furnace in which souls are wrought into new life,
but, as off a beltline, more, more senseless figures aflame.

And this insect (who is not there—
it is my own eyes do my seeing, the insect
is not there, what I see is there)
will not permit me to look elsewhere,

or if I look, to see except dulled and unfocused
the delicate, firm, whole flesh of the still unburned.

As I in hoarie Winters night
    Stood shivering in the snow,
Surpriz'd I was with sudden heat,
    Which made my heart to glow;
And lifting up a fearefull eye
    To view what fire was neere,
A prettie Babe all burning bright
    Did in the aire appeare;
Who, scorched with excessive heat,
    Such flouds of teares did shed,
As though his flouds should quench his flames,
    Which with his teares were bred:
Alas, (quoth he) but newly borne,
    In fierie heats I frie,
Yet none approach to warme their hearts,
    Or feele my fire but I;
My faultlesse brest the furnace is,
    The fuell wounding thornes:
Love is the fire, and sighs the smoke,
    The ashes shames and scornes;
The fuell justice layeth on,
    And mercy blowes the coales,
The metall in this Furnace wrought,
    Are mens defiled soules:
For which, as now on fire I am,
    To worke them to their good,
So will I melt into a bath,
    To wash them in my blood.
With this he vanisht out of sight,
    And swiftly shrunke away,
And straight I called unto minde,
    That it was Christmasse day.

Comment |

Southwell's fate is an emblem of the visionary consciousness—always in opposition to power, proposing what cannot be institutionalized, only loved. At twenty-seven, Robert Southwell returned to England from his Jesuit novitiate in France and Rome, lived seven years in clandestinity until his capture, and at thirty-four was executed on a charge of treason in 1595. His poems were not published until after his death. To Dylan Thomas, Southwell's vision afforded an illumination which he wrought into a story of incest and judgment, "The Burning Baby":

The world is ripe for the second coming of the son of man, Rhys Rhys said aloud, and the baby caught fire. The flames curled round its mouth and blew upon the shrinking gums. Flames round its red cord lapped its little belly till the raw flesh fell upon the heather. A flame touched its tongue. Eeeeeeh, cried the burning baby, and the illuminated hill replied.

To Denise Levertov, Welsh on her mother's side, the vision has been as suggestive, for her need was imperative. Southwell's image of redemption is unique in its assimilation of innocence to intensity—no figure but Blake's tiger burns so bright for us as this frying infant, and with a terrible conscientiousness—or rather, with a grimly conscious terror—Denise Levertov takes it into her own poem. For the danger to a poet is the danger of making what is unique into no more than singularity, as the danger to a poem is the danger of becoming a mere instance when ecstasy is meant.

Circumstance—the circumstance of Vietnam, the matter of the war—kindles both instance and ecstasy here: the poet's "clear caressive sight" is prepossessed by Southwell's vision, and because it is recognized as a vision, identified, Levertov's power is not engrossed by merely institutional energies. She knows as Southwell knew "how well verse and vertue sute together," and has taken great care, in the administration of her three long sentences, that the movement of the syntax athwart her burning issue is a correspondence, an analogy of her message, the hindered mind working clear, the hampered diction at last unraveled from the close-set intervals of utterance. Gathering such forces from the passing sentences, the sentence passed, Levertov speaks not of what she sees but what she cannot see, speaks of the obstacles to vision, of the blindness of power and of its doom; for "Advent," as in the Dylan Thomas quotation, is observed not only for Christmas but also for the Second Coming of the Judge at the Last Day. A profound consciousness of what is not unique, of what is not even singular, but of "more, more senseless figures aflame" charges Levertov's poem with judgment —a judgment upon herself and her country, "dulled and unfocused" with regard to the flesh of the still unburned as long as there are these cinders, this flesh on fire.

Philip
Levine

THEY FEED THEY LION

Out of burlap sacks, out of bearing butter,
Out of black bean and wet slate bread,
Out of acids of rage, the candor of tar,
Out of creosote, gasoline, drive shafts, wooden dollies,
They Lion grow.

                    Out of the grey hills
Of industrial barns, out of rain, out of bus ride,
West Virgina to Kiss My Ass, out of buried aunties,
Mothers hardening like pounded stumps, out of stumps,
Out of the bones' need to sharpen and the muscles' to stretch,
They Lion grow.

163

Earth is eating trees, fence posts,
Gutted cars, earth is calling in her little ones,
"Come home, Come home!" From pig balls,
From the ferocity of pig driven to holiness,
From the furred ear and the full jowl come
The repose of the hung belly, from the purpose
They Lion grow.

From the sweet glues of the trotters
Come the sweet kinks of the fist, from the full flower
Of the hams the thorax of caves,
From "Bow Down" come "Rise Up,"
Come they Lion from the reeds of shovels,
The grained arm that pulls the hands,
They Lion grow.

From my five arms and all my hands,
From all my white sins forgiven, they feed,
From my car passing under the stars,
They Lion, from my children inherit,
From the oak turned to a wall, they Lion,
From they sack and they belly opened
And all that was hidden burning on the oil-stained earth
They feed they Lion and he comes.

Christopher Smart

from
JUBILATE
AGNO

For the air is purified by prayer which is made aloud and with all our might.
For loud prayer is good for weak lungs and for a vitiated throat.
For SOUND is propagated in the spirit and in all directions.
For the VOICE of a figure compleat in all its parts.
For a man speaks HIMSELF from the crown of his head to the sole of his feet.
For a LION ROARS HIMSELF compleat from head to tail.
For all these things are seen in the spirit which makes the beauty of prayer.

Comment

Like Blake's prophecies, *Jubilate Agno*, Christopher Smart's interminable benedicite of the universe, is a development—a poetic development—of the translated Bible; if he wanders, if he sometimes makes no more than remarks, Smart generally recovers himself into poetry and more, as in this sublime fragment—he recovers himself from what appears obsession or paralysis, from doodling into *blessing*, a word whose root is the same as the root of the word for *action* (in all Indo-European languages, *to do* is *to revere*). Levine is content with a fragment because his own poem too is but the consummation of a series of indeterminate litanies, utterances which exalt, strangely, the actions of the poor, the broken lives of factory workers in Detroit, rural people in Kentucky and West Virginia, blacks and whites brutalized by an alien urban necessity. In both poems, the power to act and the power to bless are seen to be the one power, transfigured out of the matter of common perception into the Biblical figure of the Lion. So urgent is the deprivation in Levine's poem, so close to the surface of these starved energies is the very level of the diction, that at first we are disconcerted by the poet's words—as we are so often disconcerted by Smart's sudden confidences, his terrible intimacies. But we must learn to listen for a poet's words rather than our own. Poetry is anything but a state in which we are entitled to recognize our own words; what we *may* recognize, once the dialect of "they sack and they belly" is accommodated, is a conviction of splendor. We may understand what both poets, in the act of benediction, mean by the Lion if we consider what Yeats has said in *A Vision*:

There is always an element of frenzy and almost always delight, in certain glowing or shining images of concentrated forces; in the heart; in the human form in its most vigorous development; in the solar disc; in some symbolic representation of the sexual organs; for the being must brag of its triumph over its own incoherence.

Thrasonical the compulsion, then, yet humble, even humiliated the terms: in Levine, the victory over incoherence is won from stumps and dirt, the speech of men who have no Sacred Word; in Smart, one dare not say incoherence is defeated *à la longue*, one can only quote the man himself: "For in my nature I quested for beauty, but God, God hath sent me to sea for pearls."

John
Logan

ON THE DEATH OF KEATS (Lines for those who drown twice)   [*for John Alioto*]

—I am recommended not even to read poetry,
much less to write it. I wish I had
even a little hope.
—Send me just the words "good night"
to put under my pillow.
                          —Keats to Fanny Brawne

—I do not care a straw for foreign flowers.
The simple flowers of our spring are
what I want to see again.
                          —Keats to James Rice

I

The last month in your little Roman house
your eyes grew huge and bright as those
a gentle animal opens to the night.
Although you could not write or read
you were calmed by the thought of books
beside your bed.
(Jeremy Taylor your favorite one.
Plato and the comic Don.)
"How long is this posthumous life of mine
to last," you said.
What is a poet without breath enough?
The doctor made you swallow cupfuls of your
                    blood
when it came up
out of your rotten lungs again.
Your study of medicine
made you suffer more the movements
of your death. One tiny fish
and a piece of black bread
to control the blood

every day you died. You starved for food
and air. For poetry. For love.
(Yet you could not read her
letters for the pain.)
One night you saw a candle flame
beautifully pass across a thread from one
taper to start another.
All month you heard the sound of water
weeping in the Bernini fount.
You asked your friend to lift you up,
and died so quietly he thought you slept.
They buried you with Shelley
at a cold February dawning
beside his drowned heart
which had survived a life
and death of burning.

II

Ruth and I visited your grave
in Rome's furious August rain.
The little old Protestant plot

169

beyond the pyramid the Romans, home from
        Egypt, made
in the middle of the city.
All the names are English
which nobody knows or nods to
in the awful noise and light. Nobody speaks.
This rain springs from ancient seas
that burst
behind the bones of my face
and wash in salt tides
over the small shells of my eyes.
Since my birth
I've waited for the terror of this place.
The gravekeeper in his hooded black
rubber cloak
wades ahead of us toward your tomb.
The streams that shape and change
along the tender's rubber back
light in the thunder flash
into grotesque slits of eyes.

They see my fright. Ruth's hand
is cold in my cold hand.
You, Keats, and Shelley and Ruth
and I all drown again
away from home
in this absurd rain of Rome,
as you once drowned in your own phlegm,
and I in my poem. I am afraid.
The gravekeeper waits.
He raises his black arm.
He gestures in the black rain. The sky
moans long.
His hooded eyes fire again!
Suddenly I can read the stone
which publishes your final line:
Its date is the birthday of my brother!
"Here lies one whose name was writ in
        water."
Oh Keats, the violet. The violet. The violet
was your favorite flower.

John
Keats

—

TO AUTUMN

I

Season of mists and mellow fruitfulness,
  Close bosom-friend of the maturing sun;
Conspiring with him how to load and bless
  With fruit the vines that round the thatch-eves run;
To bend with apples the moss'd cottage-trees,
  And fill all fruit with ripeness to the core;
    To swell the gourd, and plump the hazel shells
  With a sweet kernel; to set budding more
And still more, later flowers for the bees,
Until they think warm days will never cease,
    For Summer has o'er-brimm'd their clammy cells.

II

Who hath not seen thee oft amid thy store?
  Sometimes whoever seeks abroad may find
Thee sitting careless on a granary floor,
  Thy hair soft-lifted by the winnowing wind;
Or on a half-reap'd furrow sound asleep,
  Drows'd with the fume of poppies, while thy hook
    Spares the next swath and all its twined flowers:
And sometimes like a gleaner thou dost keep
  Steady thy laden head across a brook;
  Or by a cyder-press, with patient look,
    Thou watchest the last oozings hours by hours.

III

Where are the songs of Spring? Ay, where are they?
  Think not of them, thou hast thy music too,—
While barred clouds bloom the soft-dying day,
  And touch the stubble-plains with rosy hue;
Then in a wailful choir the small gnats mourn
  Among the river sallows, borne aloft
    Or sinking as the light wind lives or dies;
And full-grown lambs loud bleat from hilly bourn;
  Hedge-crickets sing; and now with treble soft
  The red-breast whistles from a garden-croft;
    And gathering swallows twitter in the skies.

Comment |

If not despairing, then desperate in their fluttering apostrophe, Logan's "Lines for those who drown twice" (once in death, again in the realization of death: "You, Keats [. . .] / and I [. . .] drown again / away from home / [. . .] as you once drowned in your own phlegm, / and I in my poem. I am afraid.") offer that characteristic terror of process which is this poet's signal—his signal to write poems, one might say, at any rate, at any cost, to break silence by that fond utterance of the situation, that Recognition Scene he sets over and over again. Logan's ardors of dedication are of course to the *man* Keats—the Keats of the letters quoted in the epigraph and of the terrible deathbed so hallucinatorily figured in the body of the poem itself—rather than to the poet Keats, the Keats of the odes. The slow, unpersuadable triumph registered by *To Autumn* is not to be collected from an exile in the sopping Roman graveyard, but in the charged details of an intuition beyond despair, a natural history so rich and complex in its cycle as to forestall natural lament: a submission to process beyond the occasion of mourning.

Logan cannot, in his own poem, keep from casting experience in its charnel terms, for so the occasion appears to demand of him ("Since my birth / I've waited for the terror of this place"), but his capacities and his task as an artist come to his rescue here, save him from being no more than the Beddoes of the affair. For the care he takes with notation, indeed the almost musical play against each other of things heard and felt and seen ("The sky / moans long" . . . "Ruth's hand / is cold in my cold hand" . . . "The streams that shape and change / along the tender's rubber back") is warped by the end into a kind of patience: reluctantly, painfully, the revelation is given; the living poet can read the stone of the dead one. He can learn, by fraternal concession, that there is a process in that final fierce violet, as in the "furious August rain," which, if only acknowledged, which is to say *imagined*, intensely enough, can permit the kind of ultimate acceptance which so loads "To Autumn," the greatest lyric expression of patience with process in our language since Shakespeare. For all Logan's pangs, then, he achieves or is granted a patience, for that is what patience originally means: a *suffering*, here a sufferance of the worst in order to gain not the best but no more than being—that ongoing life which is writ in water indeed, "streams that shape and change," for we must alter in order to exist.

Robert Lowell

JULY IN WASHINGTON

The stiff spokes of this wheel
touch the sore spots of the earth.

On the Potomac, swan-white
power launches keep breasting the sulphurous wave.

Otters slide and dive and slick back their hair,
raccoons clean their meat in the creek.

On the circles, green statues ride like South American
liberators above the breeding vegetation—

prongs and spearheads of some equatorial
backland that will inherit the globe.

The elect, the elected . . . they come here bright as dimes,
and die dishevelled and soft.

We cannot name their names, or number their dates—
circle on circle, like rings on a tree—

but we wish the river had another shore,
some further range of delectable mountains,

distant hills powdered blue as a girl's eyelid.
It seems the least little shove would land us there,

that only the slightest repugnance of our bodies
we no longer control could drag us back.

Herman Melville

THE HOUSE-TOP

A Night Piece
(July, 1863)

No sleep. The sultriness pervades the air
And binds the brain—a dense oppression, such
As tawny tigers feel in matted shades,
Vexing their blood and making apt for ravage.
Beneath the stars the roofy desert spreads
Vacant as Libya. All is hushed near by.
Yet fitfully from far breaks a mixed surf
Of muffled sound, the Atheist roar of riot.
Yonder, where parching Sirius set in drought,
Balefully glares red Arson—there—and there.
The Town is taken by its rats—ship-rats
And rats of the wharves. All civil charms
And priestly spells which late held hearts in awe—
Fear-bound, subjected to a better sway
Than sway of self; these like a dream dissolve
And man rebounds whole aeons back in nature.*
Hail to the low dull rumble, dull and dead,
And ponderous drag that jars the wall.
Wise Draco comes, deep in the midnight roll
Of black artillery; he comes, though late;
In code corroborating Calvin's creed
And cynic tyrannies of honest kings;
He comes, nor parlies; and the Town, redeemed,
Gives thanks devout; nor, being thankful, heeds
The grimy slur on the Republic's faith implied,
Which holds that Man is naturally good,
And—more—is Nature's Roman, never to be scourged.

* "I dare not write the horrible and inconceivable atrocities committed," says Froissart, in alluding to the remarkable sedition in France during his time. The like may be hinted of some proceedings of the draft-rioters. —H.M.

Comment

The seditious tropical summers of America's cities have a literary history over a hundred years old, one discovers from this juxtaposition: views of Washington in our tranquilized, helpless sixties ("our bodies / we no longer control"), of New York during the draft riots in the Civil War which dispelled so many fond illusions ("The grimy slur on the Republic's faith"). Dissociation, severance, rifting is the theme which unites the two poets as they converge upon public outrage from such disparate private modes: Lowell the "born poet," for whom it is supremely natural to resort to or resolve upon verse, for whom the most casually observed and recounted detail ("they come here bright as dimes, / and die dishevelled and soft") can be made, by interval, phrasing, and easy rhythmic authority, to ring with the immediate symbolic assurance of connection; Melville wrenching from what must be called the originality of ineptitude an agonized yet crucial formulation of the shared discovery:

> Power unanointed may come—
> Dominion (unsought by the free)
> And the iron dome
> Fling her huge shadow . . .
> But the Founder's dream shall flee

The Founder's dream has become the American nightmare, and what makes these poets intersect for all the drastic discrepancies in their apprehension, what brings about the interference, even the *contamination*, of their courses is the stubborn consciousness that the torment of our private history and the convulsive terror of our public one mirror and enact each other; it is an inward war they wage, these exemplary sufferers, and Melville's sullen dissolution of the dream that we are "subjected to a better sway / Than sway of self" prophesies Lowell's acknowledgment that "the slightest repugnance of our bodies [. . .] could drag us back" from "another shore, / some further range" of yearned-for experience.

Political failure, psychic failure, somatic failure—the occultation of so much of what had seemed enlightened, promising, or merely a matter of piety—these lapses are in every sense *taken in*, partaken of, a kind of self-cannibalism, so that it is no longer a matter of casting blame, of scourging others, but rather of discovering a bestial energy—Melville's rats and tigers, Lowell's otters and raccoons—which forces upon us a recognition of mutual outlines, of Melville's "consciousness where more is hid than found," a world, as Lowell says, where

> . . . creatures of the night,
> obsessive, casual, sure of foot,
> go on grinding, while the sun's
> daily remorseful blackout dawns.

*William
Meredith*

EFFORT AT SPEECH

[*for Muriel Rukeyser*]

Climbing the stairway gray with urban midnight,
Cheerful, venial, ruminating pleasure,
Darkness takes me, an arm around my throat and
                                        Give me your wallet.

Fearing cowardice more than other terrors,
Angry I wrestle with my unseen partner,
Caught in a ritual not of our own making,
                                        panting like spaniels.

Bold with adrenalin, mindless, shaking,
God damn it, no! I rasp at him behind me,
Wrenching the leather wallet from his grasp. It
                                        breaks like a wishbone,

So that departing (routed by my shouting,
Not by my strength or inadvertent courage)
Half of the papers lending me a name are
                                        gone with him nameless.

Only now turning, I see a tall boy running,
Fifteen, sixteen, dressed thinly for the weather.
Reaching the streetlight he turns a brown face briefly
                                        phrased like a question.

I like a questioner watch him turn the corner
Taking the answer with him, or his half of it.
Loneliness, not a sensible emotion,
                                        breathes hard on the stairway.

Walking homeward I fraternize with shadows,
Zig-zagging with them where they flee the streetlights,
Asking for trouble, asking for the message
                              trouble had sent me.

All fall down has been scribbled on the street in
Garbage and excrement: so much for the vision
Others taunt me with, my untimely humor,
                              so much for cheerfulness.

Next time don't wrangle, give the boy the money,
Call across chasms what the world you know is.
Luckless and lied to, how can a child master
                              human decorum?

Next time a switch-blade, somewhere he is thinking,
I should have killed him and took the lousy wallet.
Reading my cards he feels a surge of anger
                              blind as my shame.

Error from Babel mutters in the places,
Cities apart, where now we word our failures:
Hatred and guilt have left us without language
                              who might have held discourse.

William Cowper

LINES WRITTEN
DURING
A PERIOD OF
INSANITY

Hatred and vengeance, my eternal portion,
Scarce can endure delay of execution,
Wait, with impatient readiness, to seize my
     Soul in a moment.

Damned below Judas: more abhorred than he was,
Who for a few pence sold his holy Master.
Twice-betrayed Jesus me, the last delinquent,
     Deems the profanest.

Man disavows, and Deity disowns me:
Hell might afford my miseries a shelter;
Therefore hell keeps her ever-hungry mouths all
     Bolted against me.

Hard lot! encompassed with a thousand dangers;
Weary, faint, trembling with a thousand terrors;
I'm called, if vanquished, to receive a sentence
     Worse than Abiram's.

Him the vindictive rod of angry justice
Sent quick and howling to the center headlong;
I, fed with judgement, in a fleshly tomb, am
     Buried above ground.

Abiram rebelled against Moses and was swallowed up by the
earth.—NUMBERS 16.

Comment

Though anything but naïve (rather, determinedly mild, resilient, and even devious) Meredith has a great gift for innocence, for the recovery of terror and joy which reside in the usual. And it is from the usual ("scribbled on the street in / Garbage and excrement") that he mounts to his moments of the genuinely vatic, inviting the mediation of the ordinary in its original sense, the sense of participation in an order, so that the poem may be an ordination. He is a poet who would single out an experience only provisionally, only to remark the more readily on its affinities with other experiences rather than on its ecstatic isolations. And on a poem's affinities with other poems—here with Rukeyser's poem of the same title, with Frost's visionary hendecasyllabic "For Once, Then, Something" which begins with the very phrase ("Others taunt me") Meredith turns to such rueful purpose, and with Auden's sestina "Paysage Moralisé" which urges, again in eleven-syllable lines, that "we rebuild our cities."

And Meredith has edited a volume of English minor poets in which he includes Cowper's famous Sapphics, one of the few cries from the heart we can hear in all the eighteenth century's good behavior. Though Cowper went mad a number of times and the rest of the time was convinced he was damned, you cannot tell it from his verse —after his first collapse, significantly, he was enabled to recover what *he* would have called his genial spirits by reading George Herbert, though he found the latter's numbers "gothick and uncouth"—for it is our fashion that the poet confess to his confusion by the vagaries of some imitative form. But as in the case of the poets named whom Meredith, in our veterinary phrase, "comes out of," there is a higher madness testified to here, the kind of truth produced by a technical opposition, a supreme friction between the violence of matter and the resistance of medium. Words are not minced, they are rather made immense by the efforts of law to accommodate their energies. Meredith's hope—it is what makes him, here, a prophet, not a preacher—is that literature intends and thereby creates a language in which we can all address one another, a discourse by which we are all members of one another, or remembered. And that language cannot be uttered unless the desperation embodied in his dark assailant, and the despair in Cowper's darker one, be also acknowledged, sustained, loved.

James
Merrill

MATINEES   [*for David Kalstone*]

A gray maidservant lets me in
To Mrs Livingston's box. It's already begun!
The box is full of grownups. She sits me down
Beside her. Meanwhile a ravishing din

Swells from below—Scene One
Of *Das Rheingold*. The entire proscenium
Is covered with a rippling azure scrim.
The three sopranos dart hither and yon

On invisible strings. Cold lights
Cling to bare arms, fair tresses. Flat
And natural aglitter like paillettes
Upon the great green sonorous depths float

Until with pulsing wealth the house is filled,
No one believing, everybody thrilled.

Lives of the Great Composers make it sound
Too much like cooking: "Sore beset,
He put his heart's blood into that quintet . . ."
So let us try the figure turned around

As in some Lives of Obscure Listeners:
"The strains of Cimarosa and Mozart
Flowed through his veins, and fed his solitary
                    heart,
Long beyond adolescence [One infers

Your elimination, sweet Champagne
Drunk between acts!] the aria's remote
Control surviving his worst interval,

Tissue of sound and tissue of the brain
Would coalesce, and what the Masters wrote
Itself compose his features sharp and small."

Hilariously Dr Scherer took the guise
Of a bland smoothshaven Alberich whose
                    ageold
Plan had been to fill my tooth with gold.
Another whiff of laughing gas,

And the understanding was implicit
That we must guard each other, this gold and I,
Against amalgamation by
The elemental pit.

Vague as to what dentist and tooth "stood for,"
One patient dreamer gathered something more.
A voice said in the speech of birds,

"My father having tampered with your mouth,
From now on, metal, music, myth
Will seem to taint its words."

We love the good, said Plato? He was wrong.
We love as well the wicked and the weak.
Flesh hugs its shaved plush. Twenty-four-
                    hour-long
Galas fill the hulk of the Comique.

Flesh knows by now what dishes to avoid,
Tries not to brood on bomb or heart attack.
Anatomy is destiny, said Freud.
Soul is the brilliant hypochondriac.

Soul will cough blood and sing, and softer
                    sing,
Drink poison, breathe her joyous last, a waltz
Rubato from his arms who sobs and stays

Behind, death after death, who fairly melts
Watching her turn from him, restored, to fling
Kisses into the furnace roaring praise.

The fallen cake, the risen price of meat,
Staircase run ten times up and down like
          scales
(Greek proverb: He who has no brain has
          feet)—
One's household opera never palls or fails.

The pipes' aubade. Recitatives. —Come back!
—I'm out of pills! —We'd love to! —What?
          —*Nothing,*
Let me be! —No, no, I'll drink it black . . .
The neighbors' chorus. The quick darkening

In which a prostrate figure must inquire
With every earmark of its being meant
Why God in Heaven harries him/her so.

The love scene (often cut). The potion. The
          tableau:
Sleepers folded in a magic fire,
Tongues flickering up from humdrum
          incident.

When Jan Kiepura sang His Handsomeness
Of Mantua those high airs light as lust
Attuned one's bare throat to the dagger-
          thrust.
Living for them would have been death no
          less.

Or Lehmann's Marschallin! —heartbreak so
          shrewd,
So ostrich-plumed, one ached to disengage
Oneself from a last love, at center stage,
To the beloved's dazzled gratitude.

What havoc certain Saturday afternoons
Wrought upon a bright young person's morals
I now leave to the public to condemn.

The point thereafter was to arrange for one's
Own chills and fever, passions and betrayals,
Chiefly in order to make song of them.

You and I, caro, seldom
Risk the real thing any more.
It's all too silly or too solemn.
Enough to know the score

From records or transcription
For our four hands. Old beauties, some
In advanced stages of decomposition,

Float up through the sustaining
Pedal's black and fluid medium.
Days like today

Even recur (wind whistling themes
From *Lulu,* and sun shining
On the rough Sound) when it seems
Kinder to remember than to play.

Dear Mrs Livingston,
I want to say that I am still in a daze
From yesterday afternoon.
I will treasure the experience always—

My very first Grand Opera! It was very
Thoughtful of you to invite
Me and I am so sorry
That I was late, and for my coughing fit.

I play my record of the Overture
Over and over. I pretend
I am still sitting in the theatre.

I also wrote a poem which my Mother
Says I should copy out and send.
Ever gratefully, Your little friend . . .

SONNET
AGAINST
RACINE'S
PHÈDRE

Dans un fauteuil doré, Phèdre tremblante et blême
Dit des vers où d'abord personne n'entend rien.
Sa nourrice lui fait un sermon fort chrétien
Contre l'affreux dessein d'attenter sur soi-même.

Hippolyte la hait presque autant qu'elle l'aime:
Rien ne change son coeur, ni son chaste maintien.
La nourrice l'accuse; elle s'en punit bien.
Thésée a pour son fils une rigueur extrême.

Une grosse Aricie, au teint rouge, aux crins blonds,
N'est là que pour montrer deux énormes tétons,
Que, malgré sa froideur, Hippolyte idolâtre.

Il meurt enfin, trainé par des coursiers ingrats;
Et Phèdre, après avoir pris de la mort aux rats,
Vient, en se confessant, mourir sur le théâtre.

Comment |

As Pound so long ago proposed, and as Picasso has so long since practiced, the surest means of appraising a convention is to face it with an alternative convention; genre is discovered by the juxtaposition of genres; the best criticism of a form is another form. To Racine's tragedy—along with *Tristan* and *Othello* the most subversive drama of passion in European letters, corrosive, preposterous, flouting certain traditions by flattering others—the drastic concision of a sonnet opposes its own mean-spirited, devastating conventions, and so accurate is the aim, so evident the target, that there will always be a time, a mood, when we feel just *this way*—bull's eye!—about the play: "A gray quivering Phaedra in a gilded chair, / Reciting verses no one understands."

Just so, quite as unfairly, as unfailingly, Merrill offers to the melodrama of his own past, to the *opera buffa* of his prospects in love and art, to the medicine-closet drama of his health and hangovers—offers the "criticism" of a sonnet sequence. Urbanity at the ready like a revolver, the poet advances into the territory ahead, the past of course, as determined to mistrust the trance, the swoon—"godgiven, elemental"—as to transcend the merely mastered:

> The point thereafter was to arrange for one's
> Own chills and fever, passions and betrayals,
> Chiefly in order to make song of them.

In these eight sonnets, everything merely *operatic* is not only the subject, but subjected to the relentless responsibility of form. In consequence, there comes the crucial realization—wry, chastened, ultimately cheering—that we are "led on" alternatively and equally by our white heats and our mere words ("both have been devices in their day"). A firescreen is not merely the flaming curtain, the destructive element, but the comfortable household convenience, and Brünnhilde's trance is as much of a convention, a device, as anapaestic trimeter. We are led on in both senses—the sense of infatuation and the sense of futurity. When the Valkyrie's baffle, "pulsing at trance pitch," proves merely portentous, Merrill turns, indeed returns, to his domestic opera, housework indeed, a hearse of a different color:

> The love scene (often cut). The potion. The tableau:
> Sleepers folded in a magic fire,
> Tongues flickering up from humdrum incident.

After all, the royal scurrility is remembered not because it is a fine and funny sonnet, but because it is a sonnet against *Phèdre*! It is an attack in the name of one convention upon the supreme example of another—of sense, which is always confined, against passion, which is always confounded. Merrill's sonnets, analogously, are not an end in themselves but an ongoing ("a nature / Which existed to be overthrown"), not a pride of place but the modesty of replacement ("tones one forgets / Even as one is changed for life by them"). "Matinees" grants the poet access to continuing powers; his reticences, his civilities, even his incivilities (that outrageous mockery of Yeats-as-Violetta: "Soul will cough blood and sing, and softer sing!") are all employed, though never overworked, in order to ballast that other impulse so searing as to be suspect, the impulse located here in *Phèdre*, in opera, in love—the impulse to reduce the merely personal to that calcined, clarified contour which consumes the accidents of time and place. This poetry articulates both impulses together, then —the impulse to reduce to anonymity, which in poetry is to be reduced to riches; and the impulse to rehearse an identity, which in life is to be reduced to tears—unites them in that living twist of idiom we call a style.

W. S.
Merwin

THE APPROACHES

The glittering rises in flocks
suddenly in the afternoon
and hangs
voiceless above the broken
houses
the cold in the doorways
and at the silent station
the hammers
out of hearts
laid in rows in the grass

The water is asleep
as they say
everywhere
cold cold
and at night the sky
is in many
pieces in the dark
the stars set out
and leave their light

When I wake
I say I may never
get there but should get
closer and hear the sound
seeing figures I go toward them waving
they make off
birds
no one to guide me
afraid
to the warm ruins
Canaan
where the fighting is

Anonymous

—

THOMAS
THE RHYMER

True Thomas lay on Huntlie bank;
    A ferlie he spied wi' his e'e;
And there he saw a ladye bright
    Come riding down by the Eildon Tree.

Her skirt was o' the grass-green silk,
    Her mantle o' the velvet fyne;
At ilka tett o' her horse's mane
    Hung fifty siller bells and nine.

True Thomas he pu'd aff his cap,
    And louted low down on his knee:
'Hail to thee, Mary, Queen of Heaven!
    For thy peer on earth could never be.'

'O no, O no, Thomas,' she said,
    'That name does not belang to me;
I'm but the Queen o' fair Elfland,
    That am hither come to visit thee.

'Harp and carp, Thomas,' she said;
    'Harp and carp along wi' me;
And if ye dare to kiss my lips,
    Sure of your bodie I will be.'

'Betide me weal, betide me woe,
    That weird shall never daunten me.'
Syne he has kiss'd her rosy lips,
    All underneath the Eildon Tree.

'Now ye maun go wi' me,' she said,
    'True Thomas, ye maun go wi' me;
And you maun serve me seven years,
    Thro' weal or woe as may chance to be.'

She's mounted on her milk-white steed,
    She's ta-en true Thomas up behind;
And aye, whene'er her bridle rang,
    The steed gaed swifter than the wind.

O they rade on, and farther on,
    The steed gaed swifter than the wind;
Until they reach'd a desert wide,
    And living land was left behind.

'Light down, light down now, true Thomas,
    And lean your head upon my knee;
Abide ye there a little space,
    And I will show you ferlies three.

'O see ye not yon narrow road,
    So thick beset wi' thorns and briers?
That is the Path of Righteousness,
    Though after it but few inquires.

'And see ye not yon braid, braid road,
    That lies across the lily leven?
That is the Path of Wickedness,
    Though some call it the Road to Heaven.

'And see ye not yon bonny road
    That winds about the fernie brae?
That is the Road to fair Elfland,
    Where thou and I this night maun gae.

'But, Thomas, ye shall haud your tongue,
    Whatever ye may hear or see;
For speak ye word in Elflyn-land,
    Ye'll ne'er win back to your ain countrie.'

O they rade on, and farther on,
    And they waded rivers abune the knee;
And they saw neither sun nor moon,
    But they heard the roaring of the sea.

It was mirk, mirk night, there was nae
        starlight,
    They waded thr' red blude to the knee;
For a' the blude that's shed on the earth
    Rins through the springs o' that countrie.

Syne they came to a garden green,
    And she pu'd an apple frae a tree:
'Take this for thy wages, true Thomas;
    It will give thee the tongue that can
        never lee.'

'My tongue is my ain,' true Thomas he said;
    'A gudely gift ye wad gie to me!
I neither dought to buy or sell
    At fair or tryst where I might be.

I dought neither speak to prince or peer,
    Nor ask of grace from fair ladye!'—
'Now haud thy peace, Thomas,' she said,
    'For as I say, so must it be.'

He has gotten a coat of the even cloth,
    And a pair o' shoon of the velvet green;
And till seven years were gane and past,
    True Thomas on earth was never seen.

---

ferlie marvel (line 2); *tett* tuft (line 7); *harp and carp*
play and recite, as a minstrel (line 17); *weird* doom (line
22); *leven* lawn (line 46); *dought* could (line 71).

Comment

It is an old story, we find it first as an encounter between Ogier the Dane and Morgan le Fay, and it has been a recurrent wonder of our poetry from Keats to Robert Graves. Merwin, who knows all about the White Goddess that Graves could have taught him, and knows too the rest no one could teach, does not invoke the ballad because of those aspects only: the magic aspects, the service poetry exacts of its adepts, the truth-telling power it bestows in return for the renunciation of rank and place, of profit and loss. Rather it is a man's relation to a transcendent mode of existence which Merwin apostrophizes in his own trance-poem: a mode of existence hinted at by the startling occurrence of the word Canaan (the Promised Land), though for Merwin that is where the fighting is—as indeed in Elfland, too "a' the blude that's shed on the earth / Rins through the springs o' that country." There is a sacramental violence, then, as well as an initiatory peace about the enterprise, and a terrible void. For there are no persons here, nor even personifications. There are presences, and they support processes which afford the speaking voice an access to prophecy, the capacity to release, just so, *the present*. It is the concern of this poem and of all Merwin's late work to resist hopes and assurances ("trying to remember what the present / can bless with"). The exultation must be *now*, it must not depend on what we have had, it must not count on what we may have; and now as we all know, is *never*—untenable, untenantable. The exultation, then, will be an ecstasy of loss, the sense of what Wordsworth called fallings from us, vanishings, yet experienced as a revelation of ourselves, a birth.

The real focus of "The Approaches," what it is approaching, is a quality of life which used to be called visionary and which Merwin would call, I think, provisional; a life which must be characterized by negatives, by what it is not, for what it is cannot be communicated to others (" 'For speak ye word in Elflyn-land, / Ye'll ne'er win back to your ain countrie' "). A phenomenology of cold and darkness, then, of loss, absence, and removal governs the imagery, even governs the tone, for a prosody of pauses, halts, and silences will let the language thicken to unwonted suspensions, enjambments which reveal, chiefly, *weight* to the ear hasty for conclusions, as they show *disparity* to the eye seeking recurrence. An irreversible course toward an undivided, unqualified life, a life entire, unmediated by any expectation but that of death; death and Childe Roland's awareness that whatever is said of such a life is not *that life*. Whence a saving tension in the poem, a continuing struggle between the cry and the crater, the hymn and the silence. As in the adventure of Thomas of Erceldoune, Scottish seer and poet, the source of Merwin's song is the deciduous life, but its seal is elsewhere, its justification is a Canaan of which the rhymer says—the modern rhymer—"I may never / get there but should get / closer and hear the sound."

Howard
Moss

WATER ISLAND   [*To the memory of a friend, drowned off Water Island, April, 1960*]

Finally, from your house, there is no view;
The bay's blind mirror shattered over you
And Patchogue took your body like a log
The wind rolled up to shore. The senseless drowned
Have faces nobody would care to see,
But water loves those gradual erasures
Of flesh and shoreline, greenery and glass,
And you belonged to water, it to you,
Having built, on a hillock, above the bay,
Your house, the bay giving you reason to,
Where now, if seasons still are running straight,
The horseshoe crabs clank armor night and day,
Their couplings far more ancient than the eyes
That watched them from your porch. I saw one once
Whose back was a history of how we live;
Grown onto every inch of plate, except
Where the hinges let it move, were living things,
Barnacles, mussels, water weeds—and one
Blue bit of polished glass, glued there by time:
The origins of art. It carried them
With pride, it seemed, as if endurance only
Matters in the end. Or so I thought.
Skimming traffic lights, starboard and port,
Steer through planted poles that mark the way,
And other lights, across the bay, faint stars
Lining the border of Long Island's shore,
Come on at night, they still come on at night,
Though who can see them now I do not know.
Wild roses, at your back porch, break their blood,
And bud to test surprises of sea air,
And the birds fly over, gliding down to feed
At the two feeding stations you set out with seed,

Or splash themselves in a big bowl of rain
You used to fill with water. Going across
That night, too fast, too dark, no one will know,
Maybe you heard, the last you'll ever hear,
The cry of the savage and endemic gull
Which shakes the blood and always brings to mind
The thought that death, the scavenger, is blind,
Blunders and is stupid, and the end
Comes with ironies so fine the seed
Falters in the marsh and the heron stops
Hunting in the weeds below your landing stairs,
Standing in a stillness that now is yours.

Matthew Arnold

—

DOVER BEACH

The sea is calm tonight,
The tide is full, the moon lies fair
Upon the Straits; —on the French coast, the
light
Gleams, and is gone; the cliffs of England
stand,
Glimmering and vast, out in the tranquil bay.
Come to the window, sweet is the night air!
Only, from the long line of spray
Where the ebb meets the moon-blanch'd
sand,
Listen! you hear the grating roar
Of pebbles which the waves suck back, and
fling,
At their return, up the high strand,
Begin, and cease, and then again begin,
With tremulous cadence slow, and bring
The eternal note of sadness in.

Sophocles long ago
Heard it on the Aegaean, and it brought
Into his mind the turbid ebb and flow
Of human misery; we
Find also in the sound a thought,
Hearing it by this distant northern sea.

The sea of faith
Was once, too, at the full, and round earth's
shore
Lay like the folds of a bright girdle furl'd;
But now I only hear
Its melancholy, long, withdrawing roar,
Retreating to the breath
Of the night-wind down the vast edges drear
And naked shingles of the world.

Ah, love, let us be true
To one another! for the world, which seems
To lie before us like a land of dreams,
So various, so beautiful, so new,
Hath really neither joy, nor love, nor light,
Nor certitude, nor peace, nor help for pain;
And we are here as on a darkling plain
Swept with confused alarms of struggle and
flight,
Where ignorant armies clash by night.

Comment |

"More and more I feel bent against the modern habit," Matthew Arnold wrote to himself, "of using poetry as a channel for thinking aloud, instead of making anything." Even here, even in his innermost resolution—or perhaps especially here, always here—the image is that of waterways, the unregarded river of our life, the channel that divides us from ourselves. "The second wave succeeds, before we have had time to breathe," Arnold said, and must have been describing the drowned man Howard Moss mourns in "Water Island"—or if not the man, then the mystery of his loss, for it is losses that the two poems grieve for, harbor, celebrate. Howard Moss yields promptly to lyric exactions, and it is not Arnold's easy sermonizing, the "thinking aloud" which made, Arnold knew, the wrong parts of "Dover Beach" so vulnerable —it is not Arnold's "eternal note of sadness" that Howard Moss makes his preference, but rather the accountability of what is seen and heard, the exactitude of the moment as it is made momentous, the sense of the site as it is . . . situated:

each perfect interval of the phrasing, the gathering voice which responds so vividly to the real impressiveness of the place, thus of the poem. Faith or friendship drowned, love jeopardized as the littoral itself—Howard Moss seizes upon the marginal things, upon what is at the brink in order to sustain his own making. His great realization, in "Water Island," is that he must submit to the facts, to the "gradual erasures of flesh and shoreline" in order to arrive at his meanings, his ironies, his truth. Reverberations are only echoes of real noises, and though he is as plangent at the Sound—for such is his gift—as Arnold on the more sententious seascape, Moss takes care to embed his sermons in stones, his symbols in extremities of observed and irreducible texture. "A history of how we live"—yes, but then: "Grown onto every inch [. . .] were living things, / Barnacles, mussels, water weeds—and one / Blue bit of polished glass, glued there by time: / The origins of art." Nothing but what we can make out of what we can see, and therefore all we have ever known.

Howard Nemerov

THE TAPESTRY

On this side of the tapestry
There sits the bearded king,
And round about him stand
His lords and ladies in a ring.
His hunting dogs are there,
And armed men at command.

On that side of the tapestry
The formal court is gone,
The kingdom is unknown;
Nothing but thread to see,
Knotted and rooted thread
Spelling a world unsaid.

Men do not find their ways
Through a seamless maze,
And all directions lose
In a labyrinth of clues,
A forest of loose ends
Where sewing never mends.

Thomas Hardy

—

A SHEEP FAIR

The day arrives of the autumn fair
    And torrents fall,
Though sheep in throngs are gathered there,
    Ten thousand all,
Sodden, with hurdles round them reared:
And, lot by lot, the pens are cleared,
And the auctioneer wrings out his beard,
And wipes his book, bedrenched and smeared,
And rakes the rain from his face with the edge of his hand,
    As torrents fall.

The wool of the ewes is like a sponge
    With the daylong rain:
Jammed tight, to turn, or lie, or lunge,
    They strive in vain.
Their horns are soft as finger-nails,
Their shepherds reek against the rails,
The tied dogs soak with tucked-in tails,
The buyers' hat-brims fill like pails,
Which spill small cascades when they shift their stand
    In the daylong rain.

POSTSCRIPT

Time has trailed lengthily since met
    At Pummery Fair
Those panting thousands in their wet
    and wooly wear:
And every flock long since has bled,
And all the dripping buyers have sped,
And the hoarse auctioneer is dead,
Who "Going—going" so often said,
As he consigned to doom each meek, mewed band
    At Pummery Fair.

Comment |

There is a truth, or perhaps but an aspect of the truth (yet as Hardy says, "Aspects are within us, and who seems / most kingly is the king"), often regarded as the one which is told most frequently in poetry— as if no one would trouble to attend to it elsewhere; the truth that *this too shall change and pass*, the truth that *what is before us now will not be before us then*, and that *we ourselves shall give way to others who will make a like observation upon us*. It is not because everyone knows this truth and has therefore consigned such knowledge to the harmless wards of poetry that the situation obtains. It is because *no one* knows it, because no one believes it, that this truth must be entrusted to poetry—for only poetry can be trusted (in the sense that "no one" trusts poetry) to deliver the message. We do not believe we are going to die, and only poems can make us acknowledge the fact that we are—only poems and our bodies when they are sick, which is why poetry is invariably associated (by the healthy) with disease. Further, we do not believe *what is now* will change, for our bodies permit no such knowledge, until they deceive us altogether and permit no other. Therefore it is the time-honored task of poetry to inform us of what we cannot otherwise endure. Poems tell us this truth by methods not available to language at its usual pressure, methods which make what we do not otherwise believe, inescapable. We call such methods form.

The three topiary stanzas of Hardy's late lyrics enforce this truth—make it not only believable but worth believing, impossible *not to believe*— by submitting their form to a presentment of reality so powerful, profuse, and yet unforced ("the tied dogs soak with tucked-in tails") that we are at first uncertain whether the presentment has indeed triumphed over the form, or whether it is the insistent "artificial" form which in music, rhythm, and interval has had the victory over the presentment of reality ("the tied dogs soak with tucked-in tails"). And the one grand, even operatic irony Hardy permits himself is so apt, so inevitable, that we cannot imagine for an instant what else it is that an auctioneer means, when he says "Going—going" except life itself, *his* life. . . .

Nemerov's lyric also engrosses our belief in the course of *its* three stanzas, but here there is not the same doubt about whether it is the presentment of reality which has subdued the form, or the form the presentment. Here we may be prompted by the poet himself, who observes —this is a late poem—"I *now* regard simplicity and the appearance of ease in the measure as primary values, and the detachment of a single thought from its ambiguous surroundings as a worthier object than the deliberate cultivation of ambiguity." So the welter of *realia* is reduced, and the poem compels our belief in its truth— its terrible truth of undersides, damaged patterns, "a world unsaid" which corresponds so preposterously to the neat side of the tapestry *we* are on—precisely by the tyranny of its form. We are made to believe what the poem declares because it has eliminated alternative possibilities: it is a spell, a rune, a conjuration. The "apparently easy" little lines, the end-stopped rhymes, and the beautiful assumption of the soothsayer's mantle ("Men do not find their ways / Through a seamless maze") knit the poem together into its unpersuadable justice, its unpardonable truth.

Adrienne
Rich

THE AFTERWAKE

Nursing your nerves
to rest, I've roused my own; well,
now for a few bad hours!
Sleep sees you behind closed doors.
Alone, I slump in his front parlor.
You're safe inside. Good. But I'm
like a midwife who at dawn
has all in order: bloodstains
washed up, teapot on the stove,
and starts her five miles home
walking, the birthyell still
exploding in her head.

Yes, I'm with her now: here's
the streaked, livid road
edged with shut houses
breathing night out and in.
Legs tight with fatigue,
we move under morning's coal-blue star,
colossal as this load
of unexpired purpose, which drains
slowly, till scissors of cockcrow snip the air.

Gerald Manley Hopkins

—

PATIENCE, HARD THING!

Patience, hard thing! the hard thing but to pray,
But bid for, Patience is! Patience who asks
Wants war, wants wounds; weary his times, his tasks;
To do without, take tosses, and obey.
    Rare patience roots in these, and, these away,
Nowhere. Natural heart's ivy, Patience masks
Our ruins of wrecked past purpose. There she basks
Purple eyes and seas of liquid leaves all day.

    We hear our hearts grate on themselves: it kills
To bruise them dearer. Yet the rebellious wills
Of us we do bid God bend to him even so.
    And where is he who more and more distils
Delicious kindness? —He is patient. Patience fills
His crisp combs, and that comes those ways we know.

Comment

In his *Dublin Notebook*, as a meditation note for the Feast of the Annunciation, March 25, 1885, Hopkins speaks of grace in a metaphor which extends his figure of honey in the waiting, firm combs: "The Virgin was full of grace, that is, she had received and stored up in her every grace offered and now overflowed in the Son . . . So the preparation for grace is grace corresponded with." The acknowledgment of pain, the preparation for grace: these are correspondences, indeed, for Adrienne Rich; to her, patience is a hard thing not because it is, literally, suffering endured, but because it is passion contained. Hopkins illustrates her case for her, makes illustrious the sure, cautious "opening-up" which *patientia* signifies. It is because life is taken in, and held there, that life can be given out, and held there. "The After-wake" so conjugates the imagery of parturition with that of severance, so confounds the lying-in with the laying-out, that we cannot readily assign the tonality, cast the role by types. It is the miracle of containment which is Adrienne Rich's stronger vessel here, the figure (waking and wake, "houses / breathing night out and in") drawn unflinchingly through the experience, sustained to the end as in Hopkins' famous sonnet, the note held until it creates a voice as exact and premonitory as that of any *sage-femme*, for the midwife is, precisely, the woman in the center for whom the natural world—"scissors of cockcrow snip the air"—constitutes the agent as well as the medium of delivery.

Jerome
Rothenberg

POLAND / 1931

"The Wedding"

my mind is stuffed with tablecloths
+ with rings but my mind
is dreaming of poland stuffed with poland
brought in the imagination
to a black wedding
a naked bridegroom hovering above
his naked bride   mad poland
how terrible thy jews at weddings
thy synagogues with camphor smells and
                almonds
thy thermos bottles thy electric fogs
thy braided armpits
thy underwear alive with roots o poland
poland poland poland poland poland
how thy bells wrapped in their flowers toll
how they do offer up their tongues to kiss the
                moon
old moon old mother stuck in thy sky thyself
an old bell with no tongue a lost udder
o poland thy beer is ever made of rotting
                bread
thy silks are linens merely thy tradesmen
dance at weddings where fanatic grooms
still dream of bridesmaids still are screaming
past their red moustaches poland

we have lain awake in thy soft arms forever
thy feathers have been balm to us
thy pillows capture us like sickly wombs +
                guard us
let us sail through thy fierce weddings poland
let us tread thy markets where thy sausages
                grow ripe + full
let us bite thy peppercorns let thy oxen's dung
                be sugar to thy dying jews
o poland o sweet resourceful restless poland
o poland of the saints unbuttoned poland
                repeating endlessly the triple
                names of mary
poland poland poland poland poland
have we not tired of thee poland no for thy
                cheeses
shall never tire us nor the honey of thy goats
thy grooms shall work ferociously upon their
                looming brides
shall bring forth executioners
shall stand like kings inside thy doorways
shall throw their arms around thy lintels
                poland
+ begin to crow

Gilgamesh washed his grimy hair, polished
    his weapons,
The braid of his hair he shook out against
    his back.
He cast off his soiled [things], put on his
    clean ones,
Wrapped a fringed cloak about and fastened
    a sash.
When Gilgamesh had put on his tiara
Glorious Ishtar raised an eye at the beauty of
    Gilgamesh:
"Come, Gilgamesh, be thou [my] lover!
Do but grant me of thy fruit.
Thou shalt be my husband and I will be thy
    wife.
I will harness for thee a chariot of lapis and
    gold,
Whose wheels are gold and whose horns are
    brass.
Thou shalt have storm-demons to hitch on for
    mighty mules.
In the fragrance of cedars thou shalt enter
    our house."

. . . .

[Gilgamesh] opened his mouth to speak,
[Saying] to glorious Ishtar:
["What am I to give] thee, that I may take
    thee in marriage?
[Should I give oil] for the body, and clothing?

[Should I give] bread and victuals?
[. . .] food fit for divinity,
[. . .] drink fit for royalty.
. . . .
[. . . if I] take thee in marriage?
[Thou art but a brazier which goes out] in the
    cold;
A back door [which does not] keep out blast
    and windstorm;
A palace which crushes the valiant [. . .];
A turban whose cover [. . .];
Pitch which [soils] its bearers;
A waterskin which [soaks through] its bearer;
Limestone which [springs] the stone rampart;
Jasper [which . . .] enemy land;
A shoe which [pinches the foot] of its owner!
Which lover didst thou love forever?
Which of thy shepherds pleased [thee for all
    time]?
Come, and I will na[me for thee] thy lovers:

Of . . . [. . .] . . .
For Tammuz, the lover of thy youth,
Thou hast ordained wailing year after year.
Having loved the dappled shepherd-bird,
Thou smotest him, breaking his wing.
In the groves he sits, crying 'My wing!'
Then thou lovedst a lion, perfect in strength;

Seven pits and seven thou didst dig for him.
Then a stallion thou lovedst, famed in battle;
The whip, the spur, and the lash thou
           ordainedst for him.
Thou decreedest for him to gallop seven
           leagues,
Thou decreedst for him the muddied to drink;
For his mother, Silili, thou ordainest wailing!
Then thou lovedst the keeper of the herd,
Who ash-cakes ever did heap up for thee,
Daily slaughtered kids for thee;
Yet thou smotest him, turning him into a
           wolf,
So that his own herd boys drive him off,
And his dogs bite his thighs.
Then thou lovedst Ishullanu, thy father's
           gardener,
Who baskets of dates ever did bring to thee,
And daily did brighten thy table.
Thine eyes raised at him, thou didst go to
           him:
'O my Ishullanu, let us taste of thy vigor!
Put forth thy "hand" and touch our
           "modesty" '
Ishullanu said to thee:
'What does thou want with me?
Has my mother not baked, have I not eaten,
That I should taste the food of stench and
           foulness?

Does reed-work afford cover against the cold?'
As thou didst hear this [his talk],
Thou smotest him and turn[edst] him into a
           mole.
Thou placedst him in the midst of . . .;
He cannot go up . . . nor can he come
           down . . .
If thou shouldst love me, thou wouldst [treat
           me] like them."

When Ishtar heard this,
Ishtar was enraged and [mounted] to heaven.
. . . .
Ishtar opened her mouth to speak,
Saying to [Anu, her father]:
"My father, make me the Bull of Heaven
           [that he smite Gilgamesh],
[And] fill Gil[gamesh . . .]!
If thou [dost not make] me [the Bull of
           Heaven],
I will smash [the doors of the nether world],
I will [. . .],
I will [raise up the dead eating (and) alive],
So that the dead shall outnumber the living!"

—Translated from
the Old Babylonian Version by E. A. Speiser

Comment

The oppositions and contraries without which there is no progression are dear to Rothenberg as well as to Blake, though the contemporary poet is less concerned to trace progressions than to let the oppositions speak for themselves. The very title of his poem sets his own birthdate against an obliterated Poland, a country, that is, of images, heterogeneous and violently yoked together, perhaps, but *named* in the one imagination, told over with the soft insistence of the dream-teller, until every instance becomes an ecstasy of enlistment, a litany: poetry's oldest recourse. The thermos bottle here and the braided armpit can survive the astonishment of their juxtaposition, for they are caught up in that one exulting voice which is propped, solaced by the naming of names, apostrophizing, weltering in the gloat of entity: poland poland poland poland poland. . . .

Gilgamesh's rejection of the lust-goddess Ishtar—but the first of countless examples in literature, with distinct premonitions, as Robert Graves has found it convenient to emphasize, of Samson in *Judges* and of Llew Llaw in the *Mabinogion* —seems here the more sophisticated text, for it takes the glorious particulars and by putting one thing after another proceeds beyond enumeration to narrative. Here ecstasy becomes instance, as in the wonderful passage where Gilgamesh itemizes the lovers of Ishtar—it is a clue to the hero's at least two-thirds humanity that he should reproach the goddess for her treatment of her consorts. No divinity, no sacred hero would hesitate a moment to leap to his destruction upon such an invitation as hers, but Gilgamesh, by precisely the kind of utterance Rothenberg is at such pains, such pleasures to create anew, manages to insert the necessary human response into what had been no more than theogony: he says no. The goddess, of course, behaves like any woman scorned and invokes her Junonian revenge, but the great thing for us here is all in the one little verse "When Ishtar heard this," for already it suggests that sequence and separation of parts which is the consequential source of all story-telling, the inception of narrative.

Rothenberg, in his pursuit of "powers, new and old, of word and song and image still here as keys for any man who reaches for them to-his-limits and in spite of cautionary schools," has come out the other side of narrative—he no longer places one utterance after another, but rather his head rings with voices, all at once, all *at one*: "my mind is stuffed" . . . and his technical responsibilities—the ambiguous enjambment, the refusal of capital letters and punctuation, the prophetic diction which is not foreseeing but fate-casting—are an approach to simultaneous apprehension. So delicate, so various, and so shrewdly observed are his specifics (a word which includes our sense of *spying* and our sense of *spice*) that he brings his poem to rest in a kind of polyphony of exultation, and by gainsaying no impulse, gains his say: at the end, and only rightly, by rapture, the cocks begin to crow.

Muriel
Rukeyser

DESPISALS

In the human cities, never again to
despise the backside of the city, the ghetto,
or build it again as we build the despised
backsides of houses. Look at your own building.
You are the city.

Among our secrecies, not to despise our Jews
(that is, ourselves) or our darkness, our blacks
or in our sexuality wherever it take us
and we now know we are productive
too productive, too reproductive
for our present invention—never to despise
the homosexual who goes building another

with touch with touch (not to despise any touch)
each like himself, like herself each.
You are this.
                     In the body's ghetto
never to go despising the asshole
nor the useful shit that is our clean clue
to what we need. Never to despise
the clitoris in her least speech.

Never to despise in myself what I have been taught
to despise. Not to despise the other.
Not to despise the it. To make this relation
with the it : to know that I am it.

Charles Baudelaire

—

LES SEPT VIEILLARDS

[*à Victor Hugo*]

Fourmillante cité, cité pleine de rêves,
Où le spectre en plein jour raccroche le passant!
Les mystères partout coulent comme des sèves
Dans les canaux étroits du colosse puissant.

Un matin, cependant que dans la triste rue
Les maisons, dont la brume allongait la hauteur,
Simulaient les deux quais d'une rivière accrue,
Et que, décor semblable à l'âme de l'acteur,

Un brouillard sale et jaune inondait tout l'espace,
Je suivais, roidissant mes nerfs comme un héros
Et discutant avec mon âme déjà lasse,
Le faubourg secoué par les lourds tombereaux.

Tout à coup, un vieillard dont les guenilles jaunes
Imitaient la couleur de ce ciel pluvieux,
Et dont l'aspect aurait fait pleuvoir les aumônes,
Sans la méchanceté qui luisait dans ses yeux,

M'apparut. On eût dit sa prunelle trempée
Dans le fiel; son regard aiguisait les frimas,
Et sa barbe à longs poils, roide comme une épée,
Se projetait, pareille à celle de Judas.

Il n'était pas voûté, mais cassé, son échine
Faisant avec sa jambe un parfait angle droit,
Si bien que son bâton, parachevant sa mine,
Lui donnait la tournure et le pas maladroit

D'un quadrupède infirme ou d'un juif à trois pattes.
Dans le neige et la boue il allait s'empêtrant,
Comme s'il écrasait des morts sous ses savates,
Hostile à l'univers plutôt qu'indifférent.

Son pareil le suivait: barbe, oeil, dos, bâton, loques,
Nul trait ne distinguait, du même enfer venu,
Ce jumeau centenaire, et ces spectres baroques
Marchaient du même pas vers un but inconnu.

A quel complot infâme étais-je donc en butte,
Ou quel méchant hasard ainsi m'humiliait?
Car je comptai sept fois, de minute en minute,
Ce sinistre vieillard qui se multipliait!

Que celui-là qui rit de mon inquiétude,
Et qui n'est pas saisi d'un frisson fraternel,
Songe bien que malgré tant de décrépitude
Ces sept monstres hideux avaient l'air éternel!

Aurais-je, sans mourir, contemplé le huitième,
Sosie inexorable, ironique et fatal,
Dégoûtant Phénix, fils et père de lui-même?
—Mais je tournai le dos au cortège infernal.

Exaspéré comme un ivrogne qui voit double,
Je rentrai, je fermai ma porte, épouvanté,
Malade et morfondu, l'esprit fiévreux et trouble,
Blessé par le mystère et par l'absurdité!

Vainement ma raison voulait prendre la barre;
La tempête en jouant déroutait ses efforts,
Et mon âme dansait, dansait, vieille gabarre
Sans mâts, sur une mer monstrueuse et sans bords!

225

Comment

Apparitions summoned before him by the witches, seven spectral kings pass before Macbeth: "Another yet! A seventh! I'll see no more. . . ." The tragic vision is the source of Baudelaire's famous shadow play, the definitive urban waste land so paradoxically fertile in modern literature, so familiar to us in Eliot's version or in Rimbaud's, in Biely's or in Joyce's, that we forget the point: the fallen city is to be redeemed, the usurped kingdom is to be purged, and the lost soul dancing on a monstrous, limitless sea, precisely because it is "wounded by mystery, wounded by the absurd," lays itself open—patient—to that other life, the life of the transfigured body, the saved society.

Already the process begins in Baudelaire, the first poet to turn the despised city into a surround acknowledged to be beautiful, or at least genuinely damned, which enables the beauty. But the process, in the procession of modernism, makes the poem itself, the *art work*, an element of alienation in the redeeming act, the soterial hope. Thus Muriel Rukeyser, in all her late work, keeps stripping the poetry away from her utterance, negating, which is the act of prose—even as she tends, in her own very splendid prose, to affirm, to celebrate, which is the act of poetry. Insofar as it protests, all utterance is prose, for it erases, denies, decries itself. Only verse can *speak in* rather than speak out, can recuperate energy by that pressure against a given (and taken) limit we call form. In another poem of the same period as "Despisals," Muriel Rukeyser says, "When I wrote of the god, / fragmented, exiled from himself [. . .] it was myself, split open, unable to speak, in exile from myself [. . .] No more masks! No more mythologies!" This is a great concession for a poet, and only the immensity of her program as a person, the vast aspiration of her utterance as a woman demanding the right to her apocalyptic body—a body which contains the world —can justify, can make illustrious her straight talking. "Not to despise the other. / Not to despise the it"—we remember that to despise means to look down upon as from a height; it is on the level that Rukeyser seeks out her condemnation ("Look at your own building. / You are the city"), even as Baudelaire, for whom a true civilization is "not in gas-lamps or in steam, but in the diminution of the traces of original sin."

Anne
Sexton

IN THE DEEP MUSEUM

My God, my God, what queer corner am I in?
Didn't I die, blood running down the post,
lungs gagging for air, die there for the sin
of anyone, my sour mouth giving up the ghost?
Surely my body is done? Surely I died?
And yet, I know, I'm here. What place is this?
Cold and queer, I sting with life. I lied.
Yes, I lied. Or else in some damned cowardice
my body would not give up. I touch
fine cloth with my hands and my cheeks are cold.
If this is hell, then hell could not be much,
neither as special nor as ugly as I was told.

What's that I hear, snuffling and pawing its way
toward me? Its tongue knocks a pebble out of place
as it slides in, a sovereign. How can I pray?
It is panting; it is an odor with a face
like the skin of a donkey. It laps my sores.
It is hurt, I think, as I touch its little head.
It bleeds. I have forgiven murderers and whores
and now I must wait like old Jonah, not dead
nor alive, stroking a clumsy animal. A rat.
His teeth test me; he waits like a good cook,
knowing his own ground. I forgive him that,
as I forgave my Judas the money he took.

Now I hold his soft red sore to my lips
as his brothers crowd in, hairy angels who take
my gift. My ankles are a flute. I lose hips
and wrists. For three days, for love's sake,
I bless this other death. Oh, not in air—
in dirt. Under the rotting veins of its roots,
under the markets, under the sheep bed where
the hill is food, under the slippery fruits
of the vineyard, I go. Unto the bellies and jaws
of rats I commit my prophecy and fear.
Far below The Cross, I correct its flaws.
We have kept the miracle. I will not be here.

Rainer Maria Rilke

___

CHRIST'S DESCENT INTO HELL

Finished at last, he escaped from that hideous
Body of suffering. Upwards. Left it.
And the darkness, alone, was frightened
And flung bats at the pale body—
In the evening, dread still fluttered
In their wings that flinched from the shock
Of that agony, grown cold. Dark nervous air
Was disheartened by the corpse; and the strong, alert
Animals of the night felt stupor and revulsion.
Perhaps his released spirit intended to stay
In the landscape, doing nothing. For the event of his suffering
Was still enough. The night-time
Presences of things seemed gentle to him,
And like a grieving space he reached out to enclose them.
But the earth, parched by his thirsting wounds,
The earth cracked open, and someone cried out in the abyss.
He, who knew of tortures, heard hell
Howling out, aching for the completion
Of his pain, in the faint hope of ending
Its agony with his, even while pain still frightened it.
And he plunged down, the spirit, with the full weight
Of his exhaustion: he walked as if hurrying
Through the surprised glances of the grazing shadows,
He lifted his eyes to Adam, hurriedly,
And ran downwards, vanished, came into view, and disappeared in the
        ruins
Of wilder depths. Suddenly (higher, higher) out over the midst
Of cries washing up, he climbed forth
To the long tower of his endurance: without breathing,
He stood there, without a railing, owner of pain. Silent.

—Translated by James Wright and Sarah Youngblood

Comment | Written shortly after the *Elegies*, this is one of the poems Rilke preferred, and he was careful to inform admirers that it was written during his stay in Ronda, Spain, in 1913—when he had withdrawn from any doctrinal association with Christianity:

You must know, Princess, that since Cordova I have become almost rabidly anti-Christian . . . One ought not to sit at this dismantled table pretending that the fingerbowls which have been left standing around are solid food! The fruit has been sucked dry and there is nothing left—to put it coarsely—but to spit out the skin. In any case, Mohammed came next, like a river through primeval rock he breaks through to the one God, to whom one can speak . . . without the telephone 'Christ,' into which people are continually shouting: *Hello, who's there?*, and no one answers.

The burden, then, of the literally harrowing figure in his poem, Christ's business is the assumption of pain, the taking to oneself of agony, the *partaking*, as at a love feast, of what can have meaning only when it is acknowledged, accepted, known, rather than put by, ignored.

To be "owner of pain" is the aspiration and the assent, so certain in all Anne Sexton's poems as well, and more than certain here, *plastic*. Though she is as reticent as Rilke about the religious significance of her Christ—hell is a museum, a place of relegation, and the dead Christ encounters not Adam, even, but a rat—Sexton's monologue is a means of knowing pain, an assent to suffering in which the very quatrains, the correct stanzas confirm what a looser prosody, a lazier diction would squirm out from under: the necessity of abasement, the craving for an access to Being in which absence ("I will not be here") is acknowledged as the image—the final image—of an absolute plentitude. To Princess Marie, Rilke wrote again at this time, "I have read Maeterlinck's book *La Mort*—it seems to me to contain a spurious calm, an induced apathy." The genuine turmoil, the "natural" agony is what he pursues, as it is this fake serenity which he abjures and which Sexton does not even allow herself to suspect: "I bless this other death," her Christ says. "Oh, not in air— / in dirt [. . .] unto the bellies and jaws / of rats I commit my prophecy and fear." Because, as Rilke said, "on earth there is spring, and in heaven refusal."

Louis
Simpson

SIMPLICITY

Climbing the staircase
step by step, feeling my way . . .
I seem to have some trouble with my vision.
The stairs are littered with paper,
eggshells, and other garbage.
Then she comes to the door.
Without eye-shadow or lipstick,
with her hair tied in a bun,
in a white dress, she seems ethereal.

"Peter," she says, "how nice!
I thought that you were Albert,
but he hardly ever comes."

She says, "I hope you like my dress.
It's simple. I made it myself.
Nowadays everyone's wearing simple things.
The thing is to be sincere,
and then, when you're tired of something,
you just throw it away."

I'll spare you the description
of all her simple objects:
the bed pushed in one corner;
the naked bulb that hangs
on a wire down from the ceiling
that is stamped out of metal
in squares, each square containing
a pattern of leaves and flowers;
the window with no blinds, admitting
daylight, and the wall
where a stream of yellow ice hangs down
in waves.

She is saying
"I have sat in this room
all day. There is a time
when you just stare at the wall
all day, and nothing moves.
I can't go on like this any longer,
counting the cracks in the wall,
doting on my buttons."

I seem to be disconnected
from the voice that is speaking
and the sound of the voice that answers.
Things seem to be moving into a vacuum.
I put my head in my hands
and try to concentrate.
But the light shines through my hands,

and then (how shall I put it
exactly?) it's as though she begins
giving off vibrations,
waves of resentment, an aura
of hate you could cut with a knife . . .
Squirming, looking over her shoulder . . .
Her whole body seems
to shrink, and she speaks in hisses:

"They want to remove my personality.
They're giving me psychotherapy
and *ikebana*, the art of flower-arrangement.
Some day, I suppose, I'll be cured,
and then I'll go and live in the suburbs,
doting on dogs and small children."

I go down the stairs, feeling my way
step by step. When I come out
the light on the snow is blinding.
My shoes crunch on ice and my head
goes floating along, and a voice
from a high, barred window cries
"Write me a poem!"

Jules Laforgue

LEGEND

Anemic pictures!
Autumnal psalm-book!
Offering my whole box of feelings and talent
To that feminine host,
A dry, persistent cough,
A woman you see on empty days,
Seated at her table, in a room that smells of winter,
Counterpoint to the great swell of the sea . . .

Romantic loves . . . where are they now?

Promiscuous embraces,
Deflowered mouths . . .
Though they are dead to music,
Still eager for the chase . . .
And still, the eyes of a beautiful, virginal soul . . .
Anyway, here she is, honoring me with her secrets.
Hearing them, I suffer more than she thinks.

"Dear lady, how is it that your clear spirit
And your glance like a steel blade
Did not cut through the pretensions
Of a mere . . . opportunist?"

"He was the first. I was alone, near the fireplace.
His horse, reined at the gate,
was uttering terrible sounds."

"I see (poor girl) . . .
And then?"

"There, look at that epilogue disguised as a sunset . . .
And then . . . O yes . . .
You see, when autumn begins
When people start to leave
The casinos
Put away the pianos.
Yesterday the orchestra attacked
Its last polka.
Yesterday the last fanfare
Went sobbing to the stations."

(How thin she is!
And what's to become of her?
You scabs of memory,
Harden . . . grow hard!)
"Well . . . in the grayness of exile
The telephone poles
Will mourn at all your funerals.
And I . . . the season wants me to go,
Winter will soon be here.
No matter . . .
Take care of yourself. Take care.

Enough, enough.
Let's not start that again.

Don't speak. Your every look is a lie.
You men are all the same.
Go now. I swear,
If I loved you, it wouldn't mean anything.

Be still.
A woman loves only once."

Ah! This is how they hurt me at last!

It is no longer the autumn,
Nor going away,
It is the sweetness of legends, the Golden Age,
Legends of women like Antigone,
A sweetness that makes you wonder
When, when did it take place?

It is legendary, like the songs
I was taught as a child.
Oh, in all the emblematic pictures,
Beasts of the earth and birds of the sky
Encircling the letters of the Missal,
Does anything bleed so much?

Bleed? I am fossilized in purest Cybelean mud!
I who, among all those Adams
And Edens, would have been as true
As the sun declining in the West . . .

—Translated by Louis Simpson

Comment /

The social furniture and the twitching prosody which serves to move it about, the little cadences of aberrant speech Laforgue worked into his studies in neurasthenia ("Yesterday the orchestra attacked / Its last polka"), must have come as a great shock to French verse, for this *façon* jeopardizes an entire literary behavior; but in English there is a convention, at least since Praed and singularized, when Laforgue was born, by Clough and Browning, of such profaned furbishings, even as there is the supreme instance of the genre in which they are deployed—the Visit of the helpless young man to the hopeless Medusa—in the fictions of Henry James.

Though Simpson cites the Laforgue poem as an ancestor of such portraits of ladies in Pound, in Eliot, and though there is some reason to see Laforgue's elliptical toughness even in *Sunday Morning* (the young man elided, the Medusa mollified), I think the force of the French poem as a manual of style is diminished, is obscured by the textures of, say, Browning—such a line as "look at that epilogue disguised as a sunset" is so perfectly carried over in Simpson's translation that one might expect to find it in *Bishop Bloughram's Apology*: "Greek endings, each the little passing-bell / that signifies some faith's about to die."

What matters more than tone, mode, or even genre—what matters most in Simpson's poem, for all its analogies of resonance with Laforgue's, is its parallel capacity to typify and characterize *period perdition*, the style-of-loss of the times. Laforgue's compulsive wraith is of course the woman we encounter so often in the early Gide (in Mme. Gide herself), in Rilke, in the paintings of Munch, and in the airless novels of D'Annunzio. She is a failed vampire, the Madonna of the Sleeping-Car, and beside her portrait Louis Simpson hangs the likeness (sparing us nothing, though he promises to) of another horror, of our own—for the failure of a woman is always the failure of a society, the collapse of a projected hope. Simpson does his creature's bidding, in a way—he writes her a poem; but the poem is an exorcism, for she too is a condemned witch ("they want to remove my personality"), his modern lady with her bored solution ("when you're tired of something, / you just throw it away"), her desperate self-cancellation ("Some day, I suppose, I'll be cured"). The poem he writes, by its refusal to fall in with itself in matters of versification, certainly sustains the sort of interest we associate with prose fiction, though the clarified ostents of a shaped experience remind us that for Simpson, in all his later work, a *poem* and a *fiction* are "as good as done," for they mean the same thing: what is made, like prayers.

L. E.
Sissman

SAFETY AT FORTY: *or* AN ABECEDARIAN TAKES A WALK

Alfa is nice. Her Roman eye
Is outlined in an O of dark
Experience. She's thirty-nine.
Would it not be kind of fine
To take her quite aback, affront
Her forward manner, take her up
On it? Echo: of course it would.

Betta is nice. Her Aquiline
Nose prowly marches out between
Two ravens' wings of black sateen
Just touched, at thirty-five, with gray.
What if I riled her quiet mien
With an indecent, subterrene
Proposal? She might like me to.

Gemma is nice. Her Modenese
Zagato body, sprung on knees
As supple as steel coils, shocks
Me into plotting to acquire
The keys to her. She's twenty-nine.
Might I aspire to such a fine
Consort in middle age? Could be.

Della is nice. Calabrian
Suns engineered the sultry tan
Over (I'm guessing) all of her long
And filly frame. She's twenty-one.
Should I consider that she might
Look kindly on my graying hairs
And my too-youthful suit? Why not?

O Megan, all-American
Wife waiting by the hearth at home,
As handsome still at forty-five
As any temptress now alive,
Must I confess my weariness
At facing stringent mistresses
And head for haven? Here I come.

Charles Cotton

—

RESOLUTION IN
FOUR SONNETS,
OF A POETICAL
QUESTION PUT
TO ME BY
A FRIEND,
CONCERNING
FOUR RURAL
SISTERS

I

Alice is tall and upright as a Pine,
White as blaunch'd Almonds, or the falling
        Snow,
Sweet as are Damask Roses when they blow,
And doubtless fruitful as the swelling Vine.

Ripe to be cut, and ready to be press'd,
Her full cheek'd beauties very well appear,
And a year's fruit she loses e'ery year,
Wanting a man t'improve her to the best.

Full fain she would be husbanded, and yet,
Alas! she cannot a fit Lab'rer get
To cultivate her to her own content:

Fain would she be (God wot) about her task,
And yet (forsooth) she is too proud to ask,
And (which is worse) too modest to consent.

II

Marg'ret of humbler stature by the head
Is (as it oft falls out with yellow hair)
Than her fair Sister, yet so much more fair,
As her pure white is better mixt with red.

This, hotter than the other ten to one,
Longs to be put unto her Mother's trade,
And loud proclaims she lives too long a Maid,
Wishing for one t'untie her Virgin Zone.

She finds Virginity a kind of ware
That's very very troublesome to bear,
And being gone, she thinks will ne'er be mist:

And yet withall the Girl has so much grace,
To call for help I know she wants the face,
Though ask'd, I know not how she would
        resist.

III

Mary is black, and taller than the last,
Yet equal in perfection and desire,
To the one's melting snow, and t'other's fire,
As with whose black their fairness is defac'd:

She pants as much for love as th'other two,
But she so virtuous is, or else so wise,
That she will win or will not love a prize,
And but upon good terms will never doe:

Therefore who her will conquer ought to be
At least as full of love and wit as she,
Or he shall ne'er gain favour at her hands:

Nay, though he have a pretty store of brains,
Shall only have his labour for his pains,
Unless he offer more than she demands.

IV

Martha is not so tall, nor yet so fair
As any of the other lovely three,
Her chiefest Grace is poor simplicity,
Yet were the rest away, she were a Star.

She's fair enough, only she wants the art
To set her Beauties off as they can doe,
And that's the cause she ne'er heard any woo,
Nor ever yet made conquest of a heart:

And yet her bloud's as boiling as the best,
Which, pretty soul, does so disturb her rest,
And makes her languish so, she's fit to die.

Poor thing, I doubt she still must lie alone,
For being like to be attack'd by none,
Sh'as no more wit to ask than to deny.

Comment /

Montaigne's translator, Lovelace's "grasshopper," Charles Cotton, the terminal *Angler*, treated his own poems in true Cavalier fashion, and never published in his life more than a few burlesques; so poised and self-possessed is this kind of writing, so *resolved*, as Cotton's title has it, that he would have been astonished, I think, not so much by Coleridge's praise as by the fact that Coleridge felt any necessity for it: "the reader sees no reason either in the selection or the order of the words, why he might not have said the very same in an appropriate conversation. . . ." For Cotton, an appropriate one is here what British law still calls a criminal one, the conversation of erotic civility. Even to our ears, the Stuart puns ("she finds Virginity a kind of ware," "she's fit to die," "as it oft falls out with yellow hair") suggest what we must always know about *light verse*, as we have come to call it—that it is "light" because of a darkness nearby, that it always suggests an alternative possibility, another level of experience besides the surface of decorum.

Sissman, too, inventories sexual likelihoods (an "Abecedarian" is not only a psalmist who begins his verses with successive letters of the alphabet, but someone who is just learning the alphabet, as well as a sectarian who despises learning and holds that even the illiterate can interpret Scripture), borrowing Eliot's famous "Grishkin is nice: her Russian eye / is underlined for emphasis," which in turn is lent by Gautier's *"Carmen est maigre, un trait de bistre / cerne son oeil de* gitana." The contemporary tyro proceeds from Alfa to (a direly punned) Omega, renouncing as he goes, and ending as he comes. The Bible calls it *knowing*, the Stuarts called it *dying*, the Victorians called it *spending*, we call it *coming*, and a hard look at the crisis in our culture suggests that it will not be long before we have a new word for orgasm —we shall call it *being*.

Gary
Snyder

PINE TREE TOPS

In the blue night
frost haze, the sky glows
with the moon
pine tree tops
bend snow-blue, fade
into sky, frost, starlight.
The creak of boots.
Rabbit tracks, deer tracks,
what do we know.

Su Tung-P'o

—

SPRING NIGHT

Spring night—one hour worth a thousand gold coins;
Clear scent of flowers, shadowy moon.
Songs and flutes upstairs—threads of sound;
In the garden, a swing, where night is deep and still.

—*Translated by Burton Watson*

Comment

The smaller the grammatical unit concerned, the greater its resistance to being stretched over a metrical boundary. Here there are no more than glowing points, embers of language in the darkness, intervals of utterance in the environing silence, the *making* of a sacred place in which the poet may then have some sort of say.

The method of a Chinese poem—the constatation of being, the utterance of a few beloved names surrounded by a mist of allusion, a mystery of silence—is or has become Snyder's too, though it is significant that he proceeds not in a garden, where the enigmas are "songs and flutes upstairs" or an empty swing in the night, but out in the woods, in winter, his only clues certain tracks in the snow and the sound of boots. The question of course is the same ("what do we know") but it is not a question asked, it is a question acknowledged, brought home, taken in. As the title of his poem indicates, Snyder is a poet who *cacuminates*, who reaches or tends to that topmost point of being where knowledge gives way to ignorance, where observation is replaced by waiting, where experience becomes expectation; as Pater says, on such occasions life itself is conceived as a sort of listening. And in such a poetry, the silences must count for a great deal—in fact the silences do all the counting, and the utterance must withdraw to the most common denominations: "sky, frost, starlight." The world becomes largely a matter of residues, of traces, to be guessed at, marveled over, left alone.

The form of this poetry—and it is all form, all *shape taken* by the senses—is not to be defined or defended by its reference to the life it seems to imitate or address, but by a style (the style of cacumination, refusing to stay *within* things, ever tending to their confines) which affords access to a world beyond itself, the world that intervenes in life, the world called religion.

*Mark
Strand*

YOUR SHADOW   (Section 4 from "Elegy for My Father")

You have your shadow.
The places where you were have given it back.
The hallways and bare lawns of the orphanage have given it back.
The Newsboys Home has given it back.
The streets of New York have given it back and so have the streets of Montreal.
The rooms in Belém where lizards would snap at mosquitoes have given it back.
The dark streets of Manaus and the damp streets of Rio have given it back.
Mexico City where you wanted to leave it has given it back.
And Halifax where the harbor would wash its hands of you has given it back.
You have your shadow.
When you traveled the white wake of your going sent your shadow below, but when you arrived
    it was there to greet you.   You had your shadow.
The doorways you entered lifted your shadow from you and when you went out, gave it back.
    You had your shadow.
Even when you forgot your shadow, you found it again; it had been with you.
Once in the country the shade of a tree covered your shadow and you were not known.
Once in the country you thought your shadow had been cast by somebody else.   Your shadow
    said nothing.
Your clothes carried your shadow inside; when you took them off, it spread like the dark on your
    past. You still had your shadow.
And your words that float like leaves in an air that is lost, in a place no one knows, gave you back
    your shadow once they were spoken.
Your friends gave you back your shadow.
Your enemies gave you back your shadow. They said it was heavy and would cover your grave.
Your wife took your shadow and said she would keep it; she died and you found it beside you on
    the bed.   Now you have your shadow.
You hated the sun because in the morning it would take your shadow and at night would give it
    back unused, untouched.
The night was good for it was your shadow and you were large surrounding the moon.
Winter took your shadow which lay like a long cape on the snow and gave it back with your
    breath.

255

When you died your shadow slept at the mouth of the furnace and ate ashes for bread.
It rejoiced among ruins.
It watched while others slept.
It shone like crystal among the tombs.
Not to be damned by abundance or uplifted by meagerness, it composed itself like air.
It wanted to be like snow on water.
It wanted to be nothing, but that was not possible.
It came to my house.
It sat on my shoulders.
Your shadow is yours.   I told it so.   I said it was yours.
I have carried it with me too long.   I give it back.

William Blake

—

from
THE FOUR ZOAS

I am made to sow the thistle for wheat; the nettle for a nourishing dainty
I have planted a false oath in the earth, it has brought forth a poison tree
I have chosen the serpent for a councellor & the dog
For a schoolmaster to my children
I have blotted out from light & living the dove & nightingale
And I have caused the earth worm to beg from door to door
I have taught the thief a secret path into the house of the just
I have taught pale artifice to spread his nets upon the morning
My heavens are brass my earth is iron my moon a clod of clay
My sun a pestilence burning at noon & a vapour of death in night

What is the price of Experience do men buy it for a song
Or wisdom for a dance in the street? No it is bought with the price
Of all that a man hath his house his wife his children
Wisdom is sold in the desolate market where none come to buy
And in the withered field where the farmer plows for bread in vain

It is an easy thing to triumph in the summers sun
And in the vintage & to sing on the waggon loaded with corn
It is an easy thing to talk of patience to the afflicted
To speak the laws of prudence to the houseless wanderer
To listen to the hungry ravens cry in wintry season
When the red blood is filled with wine & with the marrow of lambs
It is an easy thing to laugh at wrathful elements

To hear the dog howl at the wintry door, the ox in the slaughter house moan
To see a god on every wind & a blessing on every blast
To hear sounds of love in the thunder storm that destroys our enemies house
To rejoice in the blight that covers his field, & the sickness that cuts off his children

While our olive & vine sing & laugh round our door & our children bring fruits and flowers

Then the groan & the dolor are quite forgotten & the slave grinding at the mill
And the captive in chains & the poor in the prison, & the soldier in the field
When the shatterd bone hath laid him groaning among the happier dead

It is an easy thing to rejoice in the tents of prosperity
Thus could I sing & thus rejoice, but it is not so with me!

Comment /

Job in his bitterness had exclaimed, "But where shall wisdom be found? and where is the place of understanding? Man knoweth not the price thereof; neither is it found in the land of the living"—and Blake, in this supreme lyric of experience, echoes the prophetic aphorism, a *wisdom broken*, as that word indicates, before he launches, in the second part of his lamenting earth mother's song, into that sea of troubles which can be opposed only by refusing them consciousness. For to be fully conscious of *experience*—as the word's root again tells us— is to be conscious of *peril*, of suffering and anguish to a degree intolerable in history: we survive such an awareness only by apocalypse or by stupor, by the "fully creative life of god," as Northrop Frye calls it, or by the sleep of death. Our humanity, Blake is saying, is like the knight in the ballad who crosses the frozen lake and, turning round at dawn, dies of terror at realizing the danger he has incurred. How often, reading history, one thinks of that, recognizes our fate.

Like Blake's, Strand's poem is part of an emblematic trajectory, an elegy for the poet's father; but this particular fragment from the environing mosaic is also analogous to Enion's lament in its acknowledgment of the necessity to put off knowledge, to deny, to refuse, to gainsay. Strand insists on the importance, for individual survival, of rejecting that extremity of consciousness which process, which historical existence, cannot endure or transcend. He divides to conquer, divides the self to conquer the self. For "the price of experience" is negation.

Which is why Strand writes his lament not in verse but in the very dialect of negation, in prose, the one linguistic medium out to eliminate itself, to use itself up in the irrecoverable rhythms of speech rather than in the angelic measures of repetition and return. No recurrence, no refrain here, but the horror of knowing too much, of suffering more than is to be borne: "I have carried it with me too long. I give it back," Strand says to his father's "shadow," that Blakean specter of the mortal body which is life in time, or death in eternity. For once we accept, once we put on, the consciousness of others, Strand implies, we are lost. Such assumption is a "rejoicing among ruins," a "crystal among the tombs"; to say No to consciousness is the one way of evincing and yet evading the horror: negation is a mask which points to itself, advancing. The prose sentences of "Your Shadow" are for life in their refusal to recuperate a rhythm, to reverse. Strand's poem is a way of outdistancing the mind in its submission to consciousness—it is a discarding in order to pick up the blank card, the next. . . .

May
Swenson

WOMEN

Women   Or they
  should be   should be
    pedestals   little horses
      moving   those wooden
        pedestals   sweet
          moving   oldfashioned
        to the   painted
          motions   rocking
           of men   horses

      the gladdest things in the toyroom

        The   feelingly
      pegs   and then
     of their   unfeelingly
    ears   To be
  so familiar   joyfully
and dear   ridden
  to the trusting   rockingly
fists   ridden until

To be chafed   the restored

egos dismount and the legs stride away

Immobile   willing
  sweetlipped   to be set
    sturdy   into motion
      and smiling   Women
        women   should be
          should always   pedestals
            be waiting   to men

Anonymous

—

MAN, MAN, MAN IS FOR THE WOMAN MADE

Man, man, man is for the woman made,
And the woman is made for man;
As the spur is for the jade,
As the scabbard for the blade,
As for digging is the spade
    As for liquor is the can,
So man, man, man is for the woman made,
    And the woman made for man.

As the scepter's to be swayed,
As for Night's the serenade,
As for pudding is the pan,
    As to cool us is the fan,
So man, man, man is for the woman made,
    And the woman made for man.

Be she widow, wife or maid,
Be she wanton, be she staid,
Be she well- or ill-arrayed,
    Shrew, slut, or harridan,
Yet man, man, man is for the woman made,
    And the woman made for man.

Comment

From the first, May Swenson has practiced, in charms, chants, hex signs, and a whole panoply of sortilege recurrent in Western poetry since the Witch of Endor brought up Samuel, the ways not only of summoning Being into her grasp but of getting herself out of that grasp and into alien shapes, into those emblems of power most often identified with the sexual. In all her poems, especially in her iconographs—those emblem texts whose words supply their own pictures (no ideas but in forms)—she came most gratefully, most recurrently indeed, to a figure which allowed her to escape the difficulties of mere nomination (for naming frustrates knowing), and of brute mechanism (for contraption spoils identity): the figure of the centaur, which cannot be merely named for it is imaginary, and which cannot be merely artificial for it is alive. Like Virginia Woolf, whom she has riddlingly addressed ("your chaste-fierce name") in that wonderful poem "A Frontispiece," Swenson discovers her true identity when she takes to her own humanity the animal powers, when she assimilates to her female body the male significations of maker and rider. The degraded form of her centaur, of course, will be the failure of such inclusion—the hobbyhorse to which women are reduced, are constrained, "things in the toyroom."

Withering as her irony is in this grim little exercise in negative shamanism, and shaky as the pedestals are shown to be by the very shape of her poem on the page, the wonderful thing about Swenson's wisdom—the wisdom that knows we must accommodate more than ourselves in order to be ourselves—is that it joins a much earlier wisdom articulated in the old English song, a recognition that the sexes are not in subjection to one another but in confection, are *made for* each other. The phenomenologies of fitting-together, the traditional poem suggests, are various ("as the scepter's to be swayed" is surely a defeat of the phallic consciousness), but invariably suggest a final conciliation, a sense that sexuality is not a matter of poles but of congruences, of complements to be searched out in the one body and being, rather than to be located at extremes. Extremes meet: this assurance is the one Swenson shores up, her terrible tone of dismissal for "the restored egos" of sexism countered by that other tone we know from her poem "The Centaur," the tone of *self-possession*, which must mean not the "painted rocking horse" but the living animal and the loving horseman together, united, fused: "I was the horse and the rider."

Allen
Tate

WINTER MASK

[To the memory
of W. B. Yeats]

I

Towards nightfall when the wind
Tries the eaves and casements
(A winter wind of the mind
Long gathering its will)
I lay the mind's contents
Bare, as upon a table,
And ask, in a time of war,
Whether there is still
To a mind frivolously dull
Anything worth living for.

II

If I am meek and dull
And a poor sacrifice
Of perverse will to cull
The act from the attempt,
Just look into damned eyes
And give the returning glare;
For the damned like it, the more
Damnation is exempt
From what would save its heir
With a thing worth living for.

III

The poisoned rat in the wall
Cuts through the wall like a knife,
Then blind, drying, and small
And driven to cold water,
Dies of the water of life:
Both damned in eternal ice,
The traitor becomes the boor
Who had led his friend to slaughter,
Now bites his head—not nice,
The food that he lives for.

IV

I supposed two scenes of hell,
Two human bestiaries,
Might uncommonly well
Convey the doom I thought;
But lest the horror freeze
The gentler estimation
I go to the sylvan door
Where nature has been bought
In rational proration
As a thing worth living for.

V

Should the buyer have been beware?
It is an uneven trade
For man has wet his hair
Under winter weather
With only fog for shade:
His mouth a bracketed hole
Picked by the crows that bore
Nature to their hanged brother,
Who rattles against the bole
The thing that he lived for.

VI

I asked the master Yeats
Whose great style could not tell
Why it is man hates
His own salvation,
Prefers the way to hell,
And finds his last safety
In the self-made curse that bore
Him towards damnation:
The drowned undrowned by the sea,
The sea worth living for.

Fulke Greville

AN EPITAPH
UPON THE
RIGHT
HONORABLE
SIR PHILIP
SIDNEY

Silence augmenteth grief, writing increaseth rage,
Staled are my thoughts, which loved and lost the wonder of our age;
Yet quickened now with fire, though dead with frost ere now,
Enraged I write I know not what; dead, quick, I know not how.

Hard-hearted minds relent and rigor's tears abound,
And envy strangely rues his end, in whom no fault was found.
Knowledge her light hath lost, valor hath slain her knight,
Sidney is dead, dead is my friend, dead is the world's delight.

Place, pensive, wails his fall whose presence was her pride;
Time crieth out, "My ebb is come; his life was my spring tide."
Fame mourns in that she lost the ground of her reports;
Each living wight laments his lack, and all in sundry sorts.

He was (woe worth that word!) to each well-thinking mind
A spotless friend, a matchless man, whose virtue ever shined,
Declaring in his thoughts, his life, and that he writ,
Highest conceits, longest foresights, and deepest works of wit.

He, only like himself, was second unto none,
Whose death, though life, we rue, and wrong, and all in vain do moan:
Their loss, not him, wail they that fill the world with cries,
Death slew not him, but he made death his ladder to the skies.

Now sink of sorrow I who live—the more the wrong!
Who wishing death, whom death denies, whose thread is all too long;
Who tied to wretched life, who looks for no relief,
Must spend my ever dying days in never ending grief.

Heart's ease and only I, like parallels, run on,
Whose equal length keep equal breadth and never meet in one;
Yet not for wronging him, my thoughts, my sorrow's cell,
Shall not run out, though leak they will for liking him so well.

Farewell to you, my hopes, my wonted waking dreams,
Farewell, sometimes enjoyed joy, eclipsed are thy beams.
Farewell, self-pleasing thoughts which quietness brings forth,
And farewell, friendship's sacred league uniting minds of worth.

And farewell, merry heart, the gift of guiltless minds,
And all sports which for life's restore variety assigns;
Let all that sweet is, void; in me no mirth may dwell:
Philip, the cause of all this woe, my life's content, farewell!

Now rhyme, the son of rage, which art no kin to skill,
And endless grief, which deads my life, yet knows not how to kill,
Go, seek that hapless tomb, which if ye hap to find
Salute the stones that keep the limbs that held so good a mind.

Comment

"His purpose was to limn out such exact pictures, of every posture in the minde, that any man being forced, in the straines of this life, to pass through any straights, or latitudes of good, or ill fortune, might (as in a glasse) see how to set a good countenance upon all the discountenances of adversitie, and a stay upon the exorbitant smilings of chance." These, in his biography of his unpublished friend, published after his own death, are Fulke Greville's claims for Sidney's heroic examples, and they may be pressed, as well, for the examples Yeats gives in *A Vision*, where he speaks of the Dante alluded to in "Winter Mask" as a poet who has attained to Unity of Being, so that his intellect "compelled even those things that opposed it to serve, and was content to see both good and evil."

The contentment to see both good and evil—the tact, as Tate says of Dante, to "mediate between universals and particulars in the complex of metaphor," which is the tact of this poem of his, too—the humility to acknowledge that "man hates / His own salvation" is the aspiration and the conquest of Allen Tate's poem; he writes in the extremes (the poem is dated 1942) of our culture, turning to the memory *in extremis* of "the master," even as Greville, who had come to court and favor with Sidney, laments only the personal loss but lauds, rather, the Right Honorable as an example, a hope, a victory of human possibility ("Salute the stones that keep the limbs that held so good a mind").

Nature will not do, yet cannot be done without—only undone, only given away: Allen Tate's poem rejects, as all his poems reject, and all his essays, and even his novel (most of all, his novel) reject, a heretical Apocalypse, reject that compulsion of ours to cast out nature, to uproot whatever seems external to redemption, whatever might intervene between the self and salvation. He will not acknowledge an answer to his question ("Whether there is still [. . .] Anything worth living for") which does not proceed *through* nature, and he will not acknowledge an answer which does not proceed *beyond* nature—such is the sense of his astonishing acknowledgment, when it comes, at the end; the answer Yeats does not give him, but is urged or argued to give:

> The drowned undrowned by the sea,
> The sea worth living for.

The trimeters of Yeats, borrowed here and illustrated—made, I mean, illustrious in these noble, chastened stanzas—procrastinate for Tate in the same way that the sixes-and-sevens of Greville's coupled quatrains delay and then enable his wit ("that hapless tomb, which if ye hap to find"): the epitaph becomes more than a lament, a crying out upon—it becomes what the words should mean, an exploration. And the "winter mask" is seen, as Yeats says the mask of Dante, the mask of the Daemonic Man, should be seen: the persona of "simplification through intensity."

*Mark
Van Doren*

ENVY THE OLD

Envy the young who have no words at all,
And the old, for they have had them. Now by wall
In sunshine, or by candle at the dance,
Or corner-warm, stillness is circumstance
Conclusive: there they sit, and no one says
They should be heedful of bright sentences.
Their silence, innocent of insult, tries
For how much truth? Who knows? It may be wise
Or sleepy, may be amorous of death
Or heavy with remembrance—the slow breath
Of sluggards at the goal. Who blames them here
For blinking? They are privileged to peer
Past us, past Him, past anyone at all,
And speak no word, those sitters by the wall.

John Dryden

TO THE MEMORY OF MR OLDHAM

Farewell, too little and too lately known,
Whom I began to think and call my own:
For sure our Souls were near alli'd, and thine
Cast in the same poetick mold with mine.
One common Note on either Lyre did strike,
And Knaves and Fools we both abhorr'd alike.
To the same Goal did both our Studies drive:
The last set out the soonest did arrive.
Thus *Nisus* fell upon the slippery place,
Whilst his young Friend perform'd and won the Race.
O early ripe! to thy abundant Store
What could advancing Age have added more?
It might (what Nature never gives the Young)
Have taught the Numbers of thy Native Tongue.
But Satire needs not those, and Wit will shine
Through the harsh Cadence of a rugged Line.
A noble Error, and but seldom made,
When Poets are by too much force betray'd.
Thy gen'rous Fruits, though gather'd ere their prime,
Still shew'd a Quickness; and maturing Time
But mellows what we write to the dull Sweets of Rhyme.
Once more, hail, and farewell! farewell, thou young,
But ah! too short, *Marcellus* of our Tongue!
Thy Brows with Ivy and with Laurels bound;
But Fate and gloomy Night encompass thee around.

Comment / Praising his 1920 study of Dryden, T. S. Eliot commended Mark Van Doren especially for illustrating "the very wide range of Dryden's work," not just the satire (as Dryden here singles out Oldham's) but the achievement in almost every department, every species of poetry. Dryden is not suggestive, of course, Dryden is everywhere explicit; the verse says what he means it to say ("poets are by too much force betray'd") and not more than that. Yet Eliot was prophetic to admire Van Doren's breadth of response, for Dryden's is a range paralleled by Van Doren's own—in fiction, in drama, in criticism, and in almost every department, every species of poetry.

I have chosen to put with Dryden's celebrated elegy (for Mr. Van Doren determined not to specify beyond that preference for Dryden of fifty years ago—insisted, indeed, that his former student select himself out of what is not so much an embarrassment as an embodiment of riches, the *Collected and New Poems 1924–1963*) the quiet yet queerly fierce couplets which belong to the sustained middle register of Van Doren's art. On the face of it—the face of language heightened beyond mere speech ("if nothing were to be raised above that level," Dryden warns, "the foundation of poetry would be destroyed"), yet beneath any suspicion of spellbinding ("a man is to be cheated into Passion," Dryden again,

"but to be reasoned into Truth")—on the face of it, this verse appears docile enough, even decorous in diction, a convention for dealing with what a man means to say. It is a decorum, though, which admits of—which enforces—a terrible knowledge, rather a wisdom to be had only when language is "received," is handed down, and when the poet knows what is in his hands from another's ("the poet who borrows nothing from others is yet to be born," Dryden observes, "he and the Jews' Messias will come together"— very likely in the same individual). This kind of poetry, the poetry of a received idiom, is not a matter of experiment (that is merely experience) nor even of originality (that is merely a reversion to origins), but of the chastened admission that his language is the poet's fate as well as his fortune, his doom and not merely his discretion. Hence envy of the young who have no words and of the old who have had them: the silence of the old in Van Doren's poem—like Dryden's farewell to the poet his junior by some twenty-two years—is a kind of valedictory to poetry itself, the acknowledgment that utterance is no more than a task, an obligation, that the uncheated passion is all in the silence.

Dryden says, "to invent a probability and to make it wonderful is the most difficult undertaking in the art of Poetry." That is Van Doren's invention here, the invention in speech of the wonderful probability of silence.

Mona
Van Duyn

THE PIETÀ, RHENISH, 14TH C., THE CLOISTERS

He stares upward at a monstrous face,
as broad as his chest, as long as he is
from the top of his head to his heart. All her
feeling and fleshiness is there.

To be on her lap is to be all shrunken
to a little composition of bone
and held away from her upper body,
which, like an upended cot smoothed neatly

and topped with a tight, girlish bolster
of breasts, rises behind him, queer
to them both, as if no one had ever rested
upon it, or rumpled it, or pressed it.

And so it stands free of suffering.
But above it, the neck, round and wrinkling
from the downward tilt of the head it's
                    bearing,
bears the full weight of that big thing.

It is a face that, if he could see
as we are forced to see, and if he
knew, as we cannot help but know, that
his dead, dangling, featureless, granite

feet would again have to touch the ground,
would make him go mad, would make his hand,
whose hard palm is the same size
as one of his mother's tearless eyes,

hit it, since nothing in life can cure
pain of this proportion. To see her
is to understand that into the blast
of his agony she turned, full-faced,

and the face began to melt and ache,
the brows running down from their high arc
to the cheekbone, the features falling toward
                    the chin,
leaving the huge forehead unlined, open,

until, having felt all it could feel,
her face numbed and began to congeal
into this. With horror he'd have to see
the massive girl there, vapidly

gazing, stupid, stupefied.
If he said, "Willingly I dried
out of consciousness and turned to the slight
husk you hold on your knee, but let

an innocent, smaller love of a son
hold me, let not my first stone
be the heart of this great, grotesque mother.
Oh God, look what we've done to each other,"

then from the head her slow wit,
stirring, would speak, "My darling, it was not
I who belittled you, but love
itself, whose nature you came to believe

281

was pure possibility, though you came
                through
its bloody straits. And not you,
but love itself, has made me swell
above you, gross and virginal

at once. I touch what's left on my knee
with the tips of my fingers—it is an ugly,
cold corrugation. Here on my lap,
close in my arms, I wanted to keep

both the handsome, male load of your whole
body and the insupportable
complete weightlessness of your loss.
The holy and incestuous

met and merged in my love, and meet
in every love, and love is great.
But unmanned spirit or unfleshed man
I cannot cradle. Child, no one can."

John Donne

—

AIRE
&
ANGELLS

Twice or thrice had I loved thee,
Before I knew thy face or name;
So in a voice, so in a shapeless flame,
Angells affect us oft, and worship'd bee;
    Still when, to where thou wert, I came,
Some lovely glorious nothing I did see.
      But since my soule, whose child love is,
Takes limmes of flesh, and else could nothing doe,
    More subtile than the parent is,
Love must not be, but take a body too,
      And therefore what thou wert, and who,
        I bid love aske, and now
That it assume thy body, I allow,
And fixe it selfe in thy lip, eye, and brow.

Whilst thus to ballast love, I thought,
And so more steddily to have gone,
With wares which would sinke admiration,
I saw, I had loves pinnace overfraught,
    Ev'ry thy haire for love to worke upon
Is much too much, some fitter must be sought;
    For, nor in nothing, nor in things
Extreme, and scatt'ring bright, can love inhere;
    Then as an Angell, face and wings
Of aire, not pure as it, yet pure doth weare,
      So thy love may be my loves spheare;
        Just such disparitie
As is twixt Aire and Angells puritie,
'Twixt womens love, and mens will ever bee.

Comment /

The problem of apprehension, of seizure in all its senses, in all *the* senses, is what impassions Mona Van Duyn into poetry. We do not own the world we love, she laments—unless she exults—nor do the beings we long for belong to us: how much of it all are we to have on our own terms? or must it be a renunciation entirely? Her answer is that we must invent our own terms—her answer is in her form, her *façon*, her genre. That is why she chooses the wry conventions, the awry rhetoric of Donne's famous *crux* on the "disparitie [. . .] twixt womens love, and mens" to accompany her own pained rejoinder to love's oldest (or, at least, earliest) holding action: "unmanned spirit or unfleshed man / I cannot cradle."

Like Donne's high-flown inference from angelology which turns to a mannerly sneer by the time we have followed it through the rigors of its argument, the modern poem depends on a persistence of decorum, an almost obsessive observation of the rules, the pieties of versification which Mona Van Duyn yet flouts and flagellates until she has forced these domesticated quatrains of hers to sound a note she recognizes as her own. Like John Donne, too, Van Duyn is a ferocious rhymer, though one discovers it almost by accident, so intent is she on rhyming *off*, slanting away from the chime or cadence which might give comfort to the ear's ache for release. She refuses to let the mind or the ear *settle* as she chides her discourse into a present-ment of drastic order. Her poem will be, then, like Donne's much-rumpled conceit, a measure of oblique conviction in which the lacerated but laced-up rhymer administers, as she perfectly puts it, "eyeful by eyeful the exact, extensive / derangement."

Yet for all the insistence of their contraption, both these poems are pitched below the tension of the lyre, not an instrument likely to be lying around the house—there is a mocking drop in the voice, for this is parlor speech, not platform style. (And of course Donne's poem was never published in his lifetime, merely circulated—or perhaps triangulated—among friends.) Utterance of this kind tends to accommodate alternative likelihoods, to see through, if not both sides of, an argument: "The holy and incestuous / met and merged in my love, and meet / in every love," Van Duyn declares, as Donne says love will inhere "nor in nothing, nor in things / Extreme," but in the transaction between them, "it cannot be / Love till I love her that loves me." It is love's office, then, "indulgently to fit Actives to passives," he says in another place—love is the middle ground, muddied, muddled, and even, for Van Duyn, addled, enjoining a rueful wit on the abandonment of certain ecstatic possibilities. How compassionately the modern poet articulates the apprehension which the metaphysical one puts so scornfully in his own pietà, where we hardly need misread to know what he means: "at their best / women are but Mummy possest."

RINGLESS

I cannot stand the man who wears
a ring
on his little finger / a white peacock walking on the moon
and splinters of silver dust his body;
but the great man, George, cracked in half my living room
one day and I saw he was made of marble
with black veins. It does not justify the ring to say
someone gave it to you and the little finger is the only one
it will fit;
it does not justify to say Cocteau wore one
and still made the man burst silently through the mirror—
many beautiful
poems have been made with rings worn on the little finger.
That
isn't the point.
Flaubert had Jasper; Lorca had jade; Dante had amber; and Browning had carnelian;
George Washington had solid gold—even Kelly once wore a scarab there;
but I am telling you I cannot stand the man
who wears a ring
on his little finger. He may indeed
run the world;
that does not make him any better in
my needlepoint eyes.
Why
is a story.
>   There were heaps of fish lying, shimmering in the sun
>   with red gashes still heaving
>   and the mouths of medieval lovers.
>   There were gold and green glass balls bobbing in their
>   nets on the waves.
>   There were black-eyed men with hair all over their bodies

There were black-skirted ladies baking bread
and there were gallons and gallons of red wine.
A girl spilled one drop of hot wax on her lover's neck
as she glanced at his white teeth and thick arms.
There were red and silver snakes coiling around the legs
of the dancers.
There was hot sun and there was no talk.
How do I reconcile these images with our cool president,
George Washington, walking the streets? Every bone
in my body is ivory and has the word "America"
carved on it, but
my head takes me away from furniture and pewter
to the sun tugging at my nipples and trying to squeeze
under my toes.
The sun appeared in the shape of a man and he had
a ring made of sun around his little finger.
"It will burn up your hand," I said.
But he made motions in the air and passed by.
The moon appeared in the shape of a young negro boy,
and he had a ring made of dew around his little finger.
"You'll lose it," I said,
but he touched my face,
not losing a drop and passed away. Then I saw
Alexander Hamilton, whom I loved,
and he had a ring on his little finger,
but he wouldn't touch me.
And Lorca had rings around both little fingers,
and suddenly everyone I knew appeared,
and they all had rings on their little fingers,
and I was the only one in the world left without any
rings
on any
of my fingers whatsoever.
And worst of all,
there was George Washington
walking down the senate aisles
with a ring on his little finger—managing

the world,
managing *my* world.
This is what I mean—you wear a ring on your
little finger
and you manage the world,
and I am ringless
ringless . . .
I cannot stand the man who wears
a ring
on his little finger;

not even if it is you.

William Shakespeare

—

SONNET XXIX

When, in disgrace with Fortune and men's eyes,
I all alone beweep my outcast state,
And trouble deaf heaven with my bootless cries,
And look upon myself and curse my fate,
Wishing me like to one more rich in hope,
Featur'd like him, like him with friends possess'd,
Desiring this man's art, and that man's scope,
With what I most enjoy contented least;
Yet in these thoughts myself almost despising,
Haply I think on thee, and then my state,
Like to the lark at break of day arising
From sullen earth, sings hymns at heaven's gate;
       For thy sweet love remember'd such wealth brings,
       That then I scorn to change my state with kings.

Comment /

There is already an expression in the language (where else, as Diane Wakoski would ask, could it be?), a formulation which makes it not only incipient, this coupling, but indissoluble, once it is entertained—and Wakoski has seen to it that we are entertained, along with the Shakespearean obligato: what else are the man with the "ring made of sun around his little finger" and the boy with the "ring made of dew around his little finger" but entertainments, visions of this man's art and that man's scope inaccessible to the speaker save as diversions, ruined, evanescent? The expression, then, is "to suffer reverses," and it is the plot, the program of both poems to allow the impossible successes of the world to mount up, to amount to the world itself against the self, and then, at the last moment, to work the conversion, to switch the reckoning; "Haply I think on thee, and then." . . . And then none of it matters, none of it is matter, only manner, or manners: "I cannot stand the man who wears / a ring / on his little finger; / not even if it is you." Whether the other is adored or execrated is not a part of the reversal, the reversal *suffered* is because there *is* another, because the self is by that separate, sundered existence enabled to entertain, just so, the desolate or desiderated possibilities:

and suddenly everyone I knew appeared,
and they all had rings on their little fingers,
and I was the only one in the world left without any
rings
on any
of my fingers whatsoever.

This is the moment of the Shakespearean "and then," but of course for Diane Wakoski the reversal would not be suffered at this point—she substitutes her sullen "not even" for the sweet love remembered, and thereby reverses the entire course of Western love poetry, or at least one channel of the stream. Hers is a poetry of what Nietzsche predicted would be the modern voice, a poetry of *ressentiment* which does not suffer reversals gladly, though with a certain glory: "you wear a ring on your / little finger / and you manage the world, / and I am ringless / ringless . . ." Such suffering is the passion of an identifying assertion, the moment when the poet, widowed by the world and all the others in it —at least by all the other men (Flaubert, Lorca, Dante, Browning, Cocteau, George Washington —even Kelly!)—will "scorn to change my state with kings."

Robert Penn Warren

MORTMAIN

After Night Flight Son Reaches Bedside of Already Unconscious Father, Whose Right Hand Lifts in a Spasmodic Gesture, as Though Trying to Make Contact: 1955

In time's concatenation and
Carnal conventicle, I,
Arriving, being flung through dark and
The abstract flight-grid of sky,
Saw rising from the sweated sheet and
Ruck of bedclothes ritualistically
Reordered by the paid hand
Of Mercy—saw rising the hand—

Christ, start again! What was it I,
Standing there, travel-shaken, saw
Rising? What could it be that I,
Caught sudden in gut- or conscience-gnaw,
Saw rising out of the past, which I
Saw now as twisted bedclothes? Like law,
The hand rose cold from History
To claw at a star in the black sky,

But could not reach that far—oh, cannot!
And the star horribly burned, burns,
For in darkness the wax-white clutch could not
Reach it, and white hand on wrist-stem turns,
Lifts in last tension of tendon, but cannot
Make contact—*oh, oop-si-daisy*, churns
The sad heart, *oh, atta-boy, daddio's got
One more shot in the locker, peas-porridge hot*—

But no. Like an eyelid the hand sank, strove
Downward, and in that darkening roar,
All things—all joy and the hope that strove,
The failed exam, the admired endeavor,
Prizes and prinkings, and the truth that strove,
And back of the Capitol, boyhood's first whore—
Were snatched from me, and I could not move,
Naked in that black blast of his love.

Henry Vaughan

—

CORRUPTION

Sure, it was so. Man in those early days
    Was not all stone and earth;
He shined a little, and by those weak rays
    Had some glimpse of his birth.
He saw heaven o'er his head, and knew from whence
    He came, condemned, hither;
And, as first love draws strongest, so from hence
    His mind sure progressed thither.
Things here were strange unto him: sweat and till,
    All was a thorn or weed:
Nor did those last, but—like himself—died still
    As soon as they did seed.
They seemed to quarrel with him, for that act
    That felled him foiled them all:
He drew the curse upon the world, and cracked
    The whole frame with his fall.
This made him long for home, as loth to stay
    With murmurers and foes;
He sighed for Eden, and would often say,
    "Ah! what bright days were those!"
Nor was heaven cold unto him; for each day
    The valley or the mountain

Afforded vistas, and still paradise lay
      In some green shade or fountain.
Angels lay leiger here; each bush and cell,
      Each oak and highway knew them;
Walk but the fields, or sit down at some well,
      And he was sure to view them.
Almighty Love! where art Thou now? Mad man
      Sits down and freezeth on;
He raves, and swears to stir nor fire, nor fan,
      But bids the thread be spun.
I see, Thy curtains are close-drawn; Thy bow
      Looks dim, too, in the cloud;
Sin triumphs still, and man is sunk below
      The center, and his shroud.
All's in deep sleep and night: thick darkness lies
      And hatcheth o'er Thy people—
But hark! what trumpet's that? what angel cries,
      "Arise! thrust in Thy sickle"?

---

leiger resident as ambassadors (line 25);   *hatcheth* broods
(line 38).

Comment /

"There is a dim glimmering of light yet un-put-out in men," Augustine confesses, "let them walk, let them walk, that the darkness overtake them not." A fervent reader of the *Confessions*, Vaughan walks, yet is overtaken by darkness—that is the "corruption" of his title—until the trumpet of Revelations in his last line relieves him of his uncertainty:

And I looked, and behold a white cloud, and upon the cloud one sat like unto the Son of Man, having on his head a golden crown, and in his hand a sharp sickle. And another came out of the temple, crying with a loud voice to him that sat on the cloud, Thrust in thy sickle, and reap: for the time is come for thee to reap; for the harvest of the earth is ripe.

No such revelation and relief is at hand for Warren, though he sinks inward upon the mind's resources, upon the memory of pleasure, of success, even of the nonsense of the nursery, and though he too appeals to Christ to "start again." His poem, with its striking repetition of teleutons, enacts its incapacity to walk on ("I could not move"), its very stanzas mimic its stasis, its *aporia*. One of the several poems included under the general title "Mortmain," this one laments even as it celebrates, in a language quite gestural with longing ("could not reach that far—oh, cannot!": the switch from conditional to indicative is characteristic of the drama, the extremity of effort articulated), the *dead hand* of the past, the refusal of experience to cancel itself out, without the certainty or even the hope of Vaughan's angel, but merely the Augustinian question "whether that blessed life be in the memory, or no?"

For Warren the past is seen, now, "as twisted bedclothes," as a tangle of dark constraints, not as the memory of angels to be viewed at any bush or well. Indeed what is most remarkable in the contrast of the two poems taken together is the excluded middle of Vaughan's, with its tremendous memory of Genesis, of the time when man "shined a little," and its equally tremendous conviction of Revelation, that he will yet be harvested to the "countrie / Far beyond the stars / Where stands a winged Centrie"; whereas middle is all that counts in Warren's blazing immediacy of failed contact, with its blackness at the inception (not Genesis but journalism in the title, in "the abstract flight-grid of sky") and its blackness at the close (not the angel's last trump but a "black blast" of human love, mortal and futile). What signifies for Warren is the present, the impotence of memory's reach backward, of love's forward, and the moment's terrible collapse ("all things [. . .] / Were snatched from me"); what matters is, precisely, unpersuadable matter. The prayer to Christ is no more than another ejaculation, and there is no starting again, there is the paralysis, the loss *realized* in the verb's strong sense, made into reality.

298

Theodore
Weiss

THE MORAL

The dark figures, lunged ahead,
out of their twisted lust for heaven
and the stars, into the sea, into the dirt,
your father, mine, and that benighted
company,
              aeries predatory birds
grow sleek in, their lives crackling
like holocausts, the concentration camps
where tortures, working out hell's
ideology, excel,
              those, sounding
through our minds like bells, ringing us
into the catacombs that man can be,
shall they also light us, lead
us through the midnight
                        of our days?
We have warmed our hands at many strange
fires, many stray. The summer's jew's-
harp has twanged out hot blues
of some superior pain,
                        its fireflies
faraway torches for a pilgrimage
to altars crammed with sacrifices. Cries,
backs bent, glistening in bloody sweat,
to accurate, gay lashes,
                        the shriek,
a phosphorescence sizzling, of the mouse,
accomplished in the likely clutches
of the hawk, like lilies in a paradigm
spell out the moral
                  of our tale.
Whatever has happened, diverse ravishings
that love to bask in balmy weather
of a scream, the passionate failures,
the perfect despairs, these never fail us.

Dante

—

from
THE INFERNO,
Canto XXVI

Quante il villan ch'al poggio si riposa,
    nel tempo che colui che'l mondo schiara
    la faccia sua a noi tien meno ascosa,
come la mosca cede a la zanzara,
    vede lucciole giù per la vallea,
    forse colà dov' e' vendemmia ed ara;
di tante fiamme tutta risplendea
    l'ottava bolgia, sì com'io m'accorsi
    tosto che fui là 've 'l fondo parea.

Like fire-flies that the peasant on the hill
    Reposing in that season, when he who shines
    To light our world his face doth least conceal,
At the hour when fly to humming gnat resigns,
    Sees glimmering down along the valley broad,
    There, where, it may be, he toils among the vines—
So numerous the flames in the Eighth Chasm glowed
    Down all its depth, laid open to mine eyes
    Soon as I came to where the bottom showed.

—*Translated by Laurence Binyon*

Comment

Standing with Virgil on the heights above the eighth *bolgia*, that of the evil counselors, Dante compares them, for innumerable insignificance, with the fireflies seen in a valley from a hill above, though they include Ulysses; the evil counselors are enclosed each within a tongue of flame because, as in the *Epistle of James*, "the tongue is a fire, a world of iniquity: so is the tongue among our members, that it defileth the whole body, and setteth on fire the course of nature: and it is set on fire of hell."

Judgment is not, of course, what Weiss finds preferable here; rather it is that capacity, from some height of sanity, to see experience entire—"the passionate failures, / the perfect despairs" —the competence so to work the dooms and delights of human life into a complicity of utterance that there will be no disentangling of motive, no division, only the *unfailing* vision. Even Weiss's enjambments are axiological: "to bask in balmy weather / of a scream," or again, "hot blues / of some superior pain," where the line break wraps the unexpected switch in sense around the single expression. It is Dante's resource, in the very depths of hell, to illustrate, to make illustrious, the simplest, mildest experience of ordinary consciousness, as by taking notice that at dusk on a midsummer evening, *la mosca cede a la zanzara*—the fly gives way to the gnat; and then to return to Elijah's chariot. It is such an embrace of possibilities, such an amplexation that Weiss aspires to "through the midnight / of our days"; he wants a unity won or wrung from a conflicting multitude so that "all the colors drain / into one conflagration." And *the moral* is one beyond or perhaps beneath judgment, as the word itself reminds us, for it is a word that means no more than behavior, "whatever has happened." There is a site—and it is what Loyola called the "composition of place," which it is Weiss's entire endeavor to get to— where, by implication of utterance, by patterning of image and allusion, we shall unfailingly see the unity, the one life. "The Moral" is a grim approach to that grace, a confidence, in the end—in the last line—that circumstance itself will grant unity. As Weiss confirms, at his most Dantesque in an earlier poem, "they find their parts / at the moment of burning: the appropriate pain, the fitting / grief."

John
Hall
Wheelock

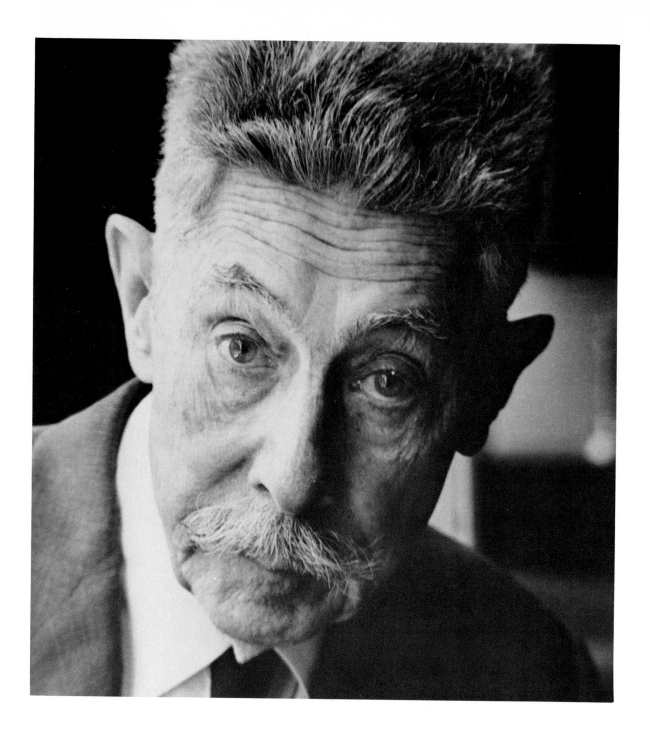

DEAR MEN & WOMEN

[*In Memory of Van Wyck Brooks*]

In the quiet before cockcrow when the cricket's
Mandolin falters, when the light of the past
Falling from the high stars yet haunts the earth
And the east quickens, I think of those I love—
Dear men and women no longer with us.

And not in grief or regret merely but rather
With a love that is almost joy I think of them,
Of whom I am part, as they of me, and through whom
I am made more wholly one with the pain and the glory,
The heartbreak at the heart of things.

I have learned it from them at last, who am now grown old
A happy man, that the nature of things is tragic
And meaningful beyond words, that to have lived
Even if once only, once and no more,
Will have been—oh, how truly—worth it.

The years go by: March flows into April,
The sycamore's delicate tracery puts on
Its tender green; April is August soon;
Autumn, and the raving of insect choirs,
The thud of apples in moonlit orchards;

Till winter brings the slant, windy light again
On shining Manhattan, her towering stone and glass;
And age deepens—oh, much is taken, but one
Dearer than all remains, and life is sweet
Still, to the now enlightened spirit.

Doors are opened that never before were opened,
New ways stand open, but quietly one door
Closes, the door to the future; there it is written,
"Thus far and no farther"—there, as at Eden's gate,
The angel with the fiery sword.

The Eden we dream of, the Eden that lies before us,
The unattainable dream, soon lies behind.
Eden is always yesterday or tomorrow,
There is no way now but back, back to the past—
The past has become paradise.

And there they dwell, those ineffable presences,
Safe beyond time, rescued from death and change.
Though all be taken, they only shall not be taken—
Immortal, unaging, unaltered, faithful yet
To that lost dream world they inhabit.

Truly, to me they now may come no more,
But I to them in reverie and remembrance
Still may return, in me they still live on;
In me they shall have their being, till we together
Darken in the great memory.

Dear eyes of delight, dear youthful tresses, foreheads
Furrowed with age, dear hands of love and care—
Lying awake at dawn, I remember them,
With a love that is almost joy I remember them:
Lost, and all mine, all mine, forever.

Thomas Moore

OFT, IN THE STILLY NIGHT

Oft, in the stilly night,
    Ere Slumber's chain has bound me,
Fond Memory brings the light
    Of other days around me:
        The smiles, the tears,
        Of boyhood's years,
    The words of love then spoken;
        The eyes that shone,
        Now dimmed and gone,
    The cheerful hearts now broken!
Thus, in the stilly night,
    Ere Slumber's chain has bound me,
Sad Memory brings the light
    Of other days around me.

When I remember all
    The friends so linked together
I've seen around me fall,
    Like leaves in wintry weather,
        I feel like one
        Who treads alone
    Some banquet-hall deserted,
        Whose lights are fled,
        Whose garlands dead,
    And all but him departed!
Thus in the stilly night,
    Ere Slumber's chain has bound me,
Sad Memory brings the light
    Of other days around me.

Comment

Moore is unheard of today, except as a genial Irishman who was good to Byron ("Damn it, Tom," Lord B. said to him as they watched a Venetian sunset, "don't be poetical!"), was admired by Scott, and was the author of a great many songs for which he wrote the tunes as well. He is forgotten for his erotic verses (written under the pseudonym Thomas Little, Esq.: "Oh! the world hath seldom heard / Of lovers who so nearly erred / And yet, who did not."), for the Byronic orientalism of *Lalla Rookh*, and—unjustly—for the pungent topical verse such as the "Copy of an Intercepted Despatch" ("I write these few lines to your Highness Satanic, / To say that, first having obeyed your directions, / And done all the mischief I could in 'the Panic,' / My next special care was to help the Elections."). We remember him for the songs like this one, all extraordinarily accomplished in versification and frequently clumsy and inadequate in their diction. In our age, as Auden says in his introduction to an anthology of nineteenth-century British minor poets including Moore, we have become so conscious of diction that if we find a poet's diction inadequate we attribute this not to carelessness but to lack of talent. Mr. Wheelock has seen through our superstition to the wonderfully crisp and decisive prosody of Moore's song, which, for all its lament and its longing, has the true joy of the spell, the incantation, the charm or *carmina*, which is what a song is—a magic which transcends behaving and becomes a kind of having instead, the possession by rather than of what cannot be had in other ways: "the light / Of other days."

Mr. Wheelock's own poem favors diction over prosody, and in its seventh, eighth, and ninth stanzas rises from ruminative utterance to a kind of triumph worthy of the Proust it makes toward in its control of tone, in its resonance of conviction. The poem abjures the stylish ease which gets (and keeps) Moore's song going, though its burden is analogous, for the sake of a speech pitched just below the tension of song, the way of talking to himself a poet lives his life to achieve, arriving at its wonderful close with what we can only call a *dying rise*: "Lost, and all mine, all mine, forever."

Richard
Wilbur

ALL THESE BIRDS

            Agreed that all these birds,
Hawk or heavenly lark or heard-of nightingale,
      Perform upon the kitestrings of our sight
      In a false distance, that the day and night
      Are full of wingèd words
                              gone rather stale,
            That nothing is so worn
            As Philomel's bosom-thorn,

            That it is, in fact, the male
Nightingale which sings, and that all these creatures wear
      Invisible armor such as Hébert beheld
      His water-ousel through, as, wrapped or shelled
      In a clear bellying veil
                              or bubble of air,
            It bucked the flood to feed
            At the stream-bottom. Agreed

            That the sky is a vast claire
In which the gull, despite appearances, is not
      Less claustral than the oyster in its beak
      And dives like nothing human; that we seek
      Vainly to know the heron
                              (but can plot
            What angle of the light
            Provokes its northern flight.)

            Let them be polyglot
And wordless then, those boughs that spoke with Solomon
      In Hebrew canticles, and made him wise;

313

And let a clear and bitter wind arise
To storm into the hotbeds
                              of the sun,
    And there, beyond a doubt,
    Batter the Phoenix out.

    Let us, with glass or gun,
Watch (from our clever blinds) the monsters of the sky
    Dwindle to habit, habitat, and song,
    And tell the imagination it is wrong
    Till, lest it be undone,
                              it spin a lie
    So fresh, so pure, so rare
    As to possess the air.

    Why should it be more shy
Than chimney-nesting storks, or sparrows on a wall?
    Oh, let it climb wherever it can cling
    Like some great trumpet-vine, a natural thing
    To which all birds that fly
                              come natural.
    Come, stranger, sister, dove:
    Put on the reins of love.

William Davenant

THE
PHILOSOPHER
AND THE
LOVER:
To a Mistress
Dying

LOVER

Your beauty, ripe and calm, and fresh
    As eastern summers are,
Must now, forsaking time and flesh,
    Add light to some small star.

PHILOSOPHER

Whilst she yet lives, were stars decayed,
    Their light by hers relief might find;
But death will lead her to a shade
    Where love is cold, and beauty blind.

LOVER

Lovers, whose priests all poets are,
    Think ev'ry mistress when she dies
Is changed at least into a star;
    And who dares doubt the poet wise?

PHILOSOPHER

But ask not bodies doomed to die
    To what abode they go;
Since knowledge is but sorrow's spy,
    It is not safe to know.

Comment

Davenant's apocryphal relations are irresistible: *said* to have been Shakespeare's godson, he *succeeded* Jonson as Laureate; knighted by Charles I, has was *reportedly* saved from execution in the Tower by Milton; having written an epic and the first English opera, he collaborated with Dryden in adapting *The Tempest* for Restoration tastes! It is a wonder such a life, and such associates, left anything over for poetry, but they did—indeed, on this evidence, for poetry of a very high order, though a very narrow range. Narrower, certainly, than Wilbur's, though it is easy to see why Wilbur prefers this obscure poem, for he says he himself is concerned "with the proper relation between the tangible world and the intuitions of the spirit. My poems assume that such intuitions are, or may be, true; they incline, however, to favor a spirituality which is not abstracted, not dissociated and world-renouncing." Precisely Davenant's concern, in his straitened quatrains—an old superstition about the soul, a fond and fearful apprehension of the body's fate, and a perfect ponderation of the speed and interval of utterance, these are the makings of his poem, which seeks no more than an accommodation with the flesh, a respite from astral certainties ("where love is cold, and beauty blind").

Wilbur, whose poem appeared the year after he had put together a superb bestiary, must have been plagued for the time by a sense of how much "meaning" we are always *adding* to the things of this world, and his poem is a momentary gaudy fit against the human habit of personifying, the custom of affabulation. Yet like Davanant—though how much more richly, the "stanzaic high-jinks," as he says, "never thought of as decorative, but rather as part of the statement"—he cannot endure a world which is not made or at least made out by the imagination, and he calls back precisely those "lies" he began by so eagerly dismissing, or rather calls upon them to "come natural." For him they do, since art is man's nature, as Burke said; and when Wilbur, who craves "that honesty which comes of the admission of doubts, contradictions, and reservations," invokes the alien world of birds to inhabit his poetic mind, his *making and shaping spirit*, by assuming the "reins of love"—constraints of that Eros Plato called the child of penury and resource—then we can ask, rhetorically, with Davenant, "Who dares doubt the poet wise?"

James
Wright

TO FLOOD STAGE AGAIN

In Fargo, North Dakota, a man
Warned me the river might rise
To flood stage again.
On the bridge, a girl hurries past me, alone,
Unhappy face.
Will she pause in wet grass somewhere?
Behind my eyes she stands tiptoe, yearning for confused sparrows
To fetch a bag of string and dried wheatbeard
To line her outstretched hand.
I open my eyes and gaze down
At the dark water.

11 I returned, and saw under the sun, that the race is not to the swift, nor the battle to the strong, neither yet bread to the wise, nor yet riches to men of understanding, nor yet favour to men of skill; but time and chance happeneth to them all.

12 For man also knoweth not his time: as the fishes that are taken in an evil net, and as the birds that are caught in the snare; so are the sons of men snared in an evil time, when it falleth suddenly upon them.

Comment / James Wright observes

that whatever the application or association of his selection from it in this instance, the King James Bible is always in his mind as a poet. Or *beneath* his mind; for in matters of phrasing, which are matters of breathing, as in manners of diction, which are manners of greeting, Wright's work is like the mysterious waters of his poem—a river that runs through all of his utterance, the Mississippi, the Ohio, or "the stream in the trees"—likely, that is, at any moment in the course of his fluent, altering discourse, to be swelled by prophetic impulse, to be immersed in that speech which is not prediction but truth-telling. The impression is that Wright himself is as helpless before the inundations of his art as the insulted and injured he writes about; he is fruitfully drowned by periodic onsets of his verbal perception, like the Nile delta. But of course this impression must be a little chastened by our sense of his immense dexterity with his own accents, the process of his own speech which, as the cunning enjambments here reveal, is ready to accommodate an astonishing range of ordinary—i.e., opaque—experience until the moment of release comes again.

Ecclesiastes is the last of the Old Testament books to be received into the Hebrew Canon, and it is of course said to be the sayings of Solomon, the harangue of a concionator who in the posture of victimization finds an ultimate wisdom. "In the destructive element immerse," might be the modern poet's exergue, even as the preacher's is "all is vanity," for it is by Wright's careful submission to these energies of dissolution and failed yearning that he wins his emblematic chapters and verses: his girl on tiptoe beside the river, "yearning for confused sparrows [. . .] To line her outstretched hand" and his own fascination with the unfathomable depths: "I open my eyes and gaze down / At the dark water." This is not one of James Wright's flood-stage poems, it is a poem of preparation, of initiatory patience, and perhaps that is why he has chosen it, for modesty is his resource, a posture of forbearance, "For man also knowth not his time . . . as the birds that are caught in the snare; so are the sons of men snared in an evil time, when it falleth suddenly upon them."

Acknowledgment is made to the following for permission to use material:

ATHENEUM PUBLISHERS, INC., and HAROLD OBER ASSOCIATES: "The Approaches" from *The Carrier of Ladders* by W. S. Merwin. Copyright © 1970 by W. S. Merwin. Appeared originally in *New Directions Annual*. ATHENEUM PUBLISHERS, INC., and CHATTO AND WINDUS LTD.: "Matinees" from *The Firescreen* by James Merrill. Copyright © 1969 by James Merrill. Appeared originally in *Poetry*. ATHENEUM PUBLISHERS, INC.: "Water Island" from *Selected Poems* by Howard Moss, Copyright © 1965 by Howard Moss. "The Pietà, Rhenish, 14th C., the Cloisters" from *To See, to Take* by Mona Van Duyn, Copyright © 1970 by Mona Van Duyn. "The Cross-Eyed Lover" from *A Joyful Noise* by Donald Finkel, Copyright © 1965, 1966 by Donald Finkel. "Giovanni Da Fiesole on the Sublime, or Fra Angelico's Last Judgment" from *Findings* by Richard Howard, Copyright © 1971 by Richard Howard, appeared originally in *Poetry*. "They Feed They Lion" from *They Feed They Lion* by Philip Levine, Copyright © 1971, 1972 by Philip Levine, appeared originally in *Kayak*. "The Vow" from *The Hard Hours* by Anthony Hecht, Copyright © 1957 by Anthony E. Hecht, appeared originally in *Hudson Review*. "The Wave" from *The Wooden Horse* by Daryl Hine, Copyright © 1965 by Daryl Hine. "The Night Mirror" from *The Night Mirror* by John Hollander, Copyright © 1971 by John Hollander, appeared originally in *The New Yorker*. "3 Stanzas about a Tree" from *The Escape into You* by Marvin Bell. Copyright © 1971 by Marvin Bell. All reprinted by permission.

CITY LIGHTS BOOKS: "Wales Visitation" from *Planet News* by Allen Ginsberg, Copyright © 1968 by Allen Ginsberg

COLUMBIA UNIVERSITY PRESS: "Spring Night" by Su Tung-P'o, translated by Burton Watson.

DELACORTE PRESS and MACMILLAN, London and Basingstoke: "Saul, Afterward, Riding East" from *Skin Diving in the Virgins* by John Malcolm Brinnin. Copyright © 1970 by The New Yorker Magazine, Inc. A Seymour Lawrence Book/Delacorte Press. Reprinted by permission.

THE DIAL PRESS and JEROME ROTHENBERG: "Poland/1931 (The Wedding)" from *Poems for the Game of Silence 1960–1970* by Jerome Rothenberg. Copyright © 1960, 1964, 1966, 1967, 1968, 1969, 1970, 1971 by Jerome Rothenberg. Reprinted by permission.

DOUBLEDAY & CO., INC.: "Ringless" from *Inside the Blood Factory* by Diane Wakoski, Copyright © 1968 by Diane Wakoski. "The Copulating Gods" from *Midnight Was*

My Cry by Carolyn Kizer, Copyright © 1971 by Carolyn Kizer.

E. P. DUTTON & CO., INC., and INTERNATIONAL FAMOUS AGENCY: "Soonest Mended" from the book *The Double Dream of Spring* by John Ashbery. Copyright © 1970, 1969, 1968, 1967, 1966 by John Ashbery. E. P. DUTTON & CO., INC.: "On the Death of Keats" from the book *The Zigzag Walk* by John Logan. Copyright © 1963, 1964, 1965, 1966, 1967, 1968, 1969 by John Logan. Published by E. P. Dutton & Co., Inc., and used with permission.

FARRAR, STRAUS & GIROUX, INC., and FABER AND FABER LIMITED: "July in Washington" by Robert Lowell from *For the Union Dead* by Robert Lowell, Copyright © 1964 by Robert Lowell. FARRAR, STRAUS & GIROUX, INC.: "In the Waiting Room" by Elizabeth Bishop, Copyright © 1971 by Elizabeth Bishop, first published in *The New Yorker*. Reprinted by permission.

GROVE PRESS, INC.: "My Polish Grandma" from *Variety Photoplays* by Edward Field, Copyright © 1967 by Edward Field. Reprinted by permission of Grove Press, Inc.

HARCOURT BRACE JOVANOVICH, INC., and FABER AND FABER LIMITED: "All These Birds" by Richard Wilbur from *Things of This World* (in England *Poems 1943– 1956*) Copyright 1955 by Richard Wilbur. Reprinted by permission.

HARPER & ROW, PUBLISHERS, INC., and OXFORD UNIVERSITY PRESS: "Simplicity" from *Adventures of the Letter I* by Louis Simpson, Copyright © 1968 by Louis Simpson. Reprinted by permission.

HARVARD UNIVERSITY PRESS: Reprinted by permission of the publishers and the Trustees of Amherst College from Thomas H. Johnson, Editor, *The Poems of Emily Dickinson*, Cambridge, Mass.: The Belknap Press of Harvard University Press, Copyright, 1951, 1955, by The President and Fellows of Harvard College.

HILL AND WANG and MARK VAN DOREN: "Envy the Old" from *Collected and New Poems 1924–1963* by Mark Van Doren, Copyright © 1963 by Mark Van Doren. Reprinted by permission of Hill and Wang, a division of Farrar, Straus & Giroux, Inc., and Mark Van Doren.

DANIEL HOFFMAN: "The City of Satisfactions" © 1963 by Daniel Hoffman, used with the permission of the author.

HOLT, RINEHART AND WINSTON, INC.: "My Olson Elegy" from *Lost Originals* by Irving Feldman. Copyright © 1971, 1972 by Irving Feldman. Reprinted by permission of Holt, Rinehart and Winston, Inc.

To invent a probability & make it workable...

John Snyder
(is the most difficult undertaking in the art of mystery)